BUT GOD KEPT ME

SHAMIKA KING

But God Kept Me

Published by Nourish Inspirations, LLC

Copyright © 2018 by Shamika King

ISBN No. 9781719415774

Table of Contents

Acknowledgements

All Glory to God! Thank You Jesus!

I will praise the Lord at all times. I will constantly speak his praises. -Psalms 34:1 NLT

Special Thanks to my Aunt, Venus King; Thank You for your wise advice and inspiring me to be diverse as I continue to write freely. I appreciate you and I love you.

Chapter One

I was so excited for my 23rd birthday on the outside but on the inside, I felt overwhelmed and drained. I was excited about what I would wear, how I would look and where this special event would take place. I was all over the place, unstable and indecisive about a lot of things. My birthday only added to it. I never did anything for my past birthdays, so I really looked forward to this one being special. After all the excitement, shopping and finding the perfect outfit, I went to my mother's house.

Although I had my own place, I was always at her house. Me and my mother didn't have the best relationship. To be honest we didn't quite have a relationship at all. My mother was very overprotective with me. I always felt like she disliked me and had something against me. I would always have flashbacks about how she would come home from work angry with herself and take her frustrations out on me.

It seemed to me, like I was always her target. Although I had a disrespectful mouth, most times I didn't do anything, yet she would still pick with me. I loved being at my mother's house. Me and her never really spoke much but for some reason I loved being around her. There where many things she did to me unintentionally. The wound was still so fresh… the pain lingered.

My birthday came and went. The thought itself was provocative how I wanted to celebrate. However, it turned out to be just another day. As time passed by, there was an unperceived feeling within me that I couldn't deviate. I started thinking about how I wanted to go to church. I never had a thought like that cross my mind. I never been to church, neither was I brought up around family members who discussed anything related to church.

This thought didn't just come out of nowhere and went away like any other thought, it was heavy on my mind. At my workplace, one of my coworkers attended church frequently. I didn't really know much about her, but I figured it wouldn't hurt to ask about church. She explained somethings about the holy spirit. Although, I didn't understand anything she was saying to me, it's as if she was speaking to that unperceived feeling on the inside of me.

She didn't hesitate to invite me out to her church. She provided me with the location and specific times that her church service started. I thanked her, I was curious to attend this upcoming Sunday. Immediately Sunday morning approached. I laid in my bed and that same feeling came over me again.

I begin to feel anxious and afraid at the same time. I didn't know what was going on, but I really wanted to know. I finally got up determined that I was going to a place called church. I got me, and my son dressed quickly as we headed straight to my coworker's church. When I made it there, I didn't quite understand what the preacher was talking about.

I still sat through the service until it was over. Once I returned home, I started feeling like something was missing. I didn't know what was going on, first the strange feeling and now the missing feeling. During this time in my life, I didn't know how to pray. Neither did I know anything about God.

I tried to not think about these strange feelings that I felt. However, I was still curious to know what it was.
One morning, while dropping my son off to school Mrs. Eternal, his teacher asked to speak with me. She really wanted to talk to me, so I waited aside. I figured it was concerning my son.

Mrs. Eternal looked me directly in my eyes.

"I can see God in you. God is trying to get your attention. You are tired from a lot of things and you want more of God. It's alright if you don't know, you don't have to be afraid. He will keep you and guide you" she said.

Now I didn't know this woman from a can of paint, all I knew was that she was my son head start teacher.

"You should visit my church on the southside of Chicago sometime. I always sit in the 5th row to your right from the entrance" she said.

"Ok" I responded.

Leaving my son school, I was trying to figure out how did she know how I was feeling on the inside.

"what in the world is going on?" I thought to myself.

I kept thinking about how she said God was trying to get my attention. I would think on and off that maybe this feeling that came over me out of nowhere could be God. For the rest of the week, I did nothing but go to work and come straight home. I would lay in my bed and cry just thinking about my life. I would think about all the things that didn't go right and all the things I was wrapped up in.

The more I tried to make sense of it all, the more it kept getting worse. It was a terrible feeling and all I desired was to get help. I was tired of living the way I was living. Deep down inside I knew it had to be another way. I was tired of the pain that constantly lingered within me.

I was full of anger and I wanted to be free from the negative thoughts that filled my mind. I was disintegrated, and my heart was afflicted. All I wanted was to be redeemed from my past and my ways. When Sunday morning came around, I was up and ready for service. It amazed me how every time I would get up for church, I would always feel exhausted.

However, there was a hunger and thirst deep within me to attend church and so I did. On my first visit to Mrs. Eternal's church, that unperceived feeling came over me again. I can't really explain what it felt like. I know that it was a warm, comforting feeling. I sat up and listened to every word the Bishop was preaching. This man preached my entire life and he didn't even know me.

Tears flowed from my eyes as I begin to wonder;

"how does this man know what I'm feeling and going through right now?" I thought to myself.

While crying I looked around, I was ashamed because I never cried in front of others before. When I cried, I cried to myself alone in my bedroom and no one ever knew. This was my second time visiting a church and my first time crying around a bunch of people that I didn't know. This was a different type of cry though. Normally when I cry at night to myself, I'm able to control my tears.

For some odd reason, this time I was incapable of my tears. At the end of service, the Bishop was calling for anyone who was willing to give their life to Jesus Christ. I wanted to get up so bad and give my life to Jesus. I didn't know much about what that even meant. I didn't even know who Jesus Christ was.

There was something in me that felt like I had been set on fire. I wanted to know who this Jesus guy was. I really wanted to get up and give my life to him, yet I couldn't move. When I made it back home, all I could think about was how that Bishop knew exactly what I was going through. I was inquisitive to get up and attend service again the following Sunday.

"If that Bishop says anything else about me and what I'm going through, I am giving my life to Jesus Christ" I said to myself.

Through the week I was afire about attending service on Sunday. I was resolute that I was going to give my life to Christ. During this time, I was only 23 years old. I didn't know Jesus, yet I wanted to know him. I was already yearning for more of him.

When Sunday came around, I was up, prepared and headed out to church. I would always sit next to Mrs. Eternal. I felt comfortable next to her for some reason. She was always full of joy and never was she ashamed to praise God. I can tell that she really loved God and I desired to feel the same way when it came to him.

"Do you have a bible?" she asked.

"No, I don't. where can I find one?" I said.

"They sell bibles here in the bookstore but don't worry, I have one for you at home. I will bring it with me to church next Sunday. You can have it" she said.

"Ok. Thank You" I replied.

There was never a dull moment at this church. Every time the bishop preached the Word of God, I felt that warm, comforting feeling repeatedly. I wanted to cry out to God, but I was penitent. I felt that because I really didn't know Jesus, who was I to praise and worship him. Instead of me praising and worshipping God, I watch everyone else.

Service was almost over and again, it was that time for people to make that choice and give their life to Christ. I knew in my mind that I was going to get up and go but once again, I couldn't move. I begin to think about what my family would think of me. I thought about what my ex-boyfriend would think of me and how everyone would talk about me. I was indecisive and once again I didn't give me life to Christ.

I went straight home after service, laid in my bed and wailed.

"why can't I do it? why is it so hard? why did I begin to think about things and people that doesn't even matter? I don't want to be afraid. Jesus, whoever you are; Can you please be with me next Sunday? All I want to do is get up and come to you" I said aloud.

For the rest of the week, I went to work in silence, did my job and came straight home. Sunday came around again, it was January 20, 2013. I was up and ready for service bound to give my life to Christ. I remember wearing a pink and white strip shirt, a black hat, black wedges and black pants. This time I didn't sit by Mrs. Eternal, I sat closer to the stage.

The Bishop begin to preach my entire life once again. This time I didn't wonder how he knew, instead I listened to every word. He pointed in the area I was sitting in.

"It's someone in this section that wants to give their life to Christ but you're afraid of what others might think of you. I don't know who you are but I'm not ending this service until you come".

"That's it!" I said to myself.

I got up shaking with tears pouring from my eyes as I nervously stumbled to give my life to Christ. This was my first time getting baptized. I was nervous, and I really didn't know what to expect. After the baptism, I went into this class with everyone else who gave their life to Christ as well. We all begin to praise God, I was still afraid to open my mouth, so I whispered as I praised him. While leaving out I ran into Mrs. Eternal, she looked after my son for me until I was done.

"Praise God! I knew it was going to happen when I first saw you. Jesus loves you! Praise God!" she said.

She handed me the bible she promised to give to me and gave me a hug as we departed. From that day forward, everything started to go wrong for me. There was more bad than good taking place in my life. I was confused, I thought that once I got baptized everything would go away. In

February 2013, I lost my job at the movie theatre that I worked at for almost 3 years.

In March 2013, Due to me being naïve, I lost my first car. I was confined for the first time in my life. I was devastated, and I didn't understand what was going on. After a while, I stopped attending church. I refused to get on the bus to travel south.

In April 2013, I was finally able to find a job located in the downtown area of Chicago. I loved it at this place. Everyone was nice but only for a while though. The manager started acting weird and she treated me unfair. Every time I went to work, tension filled the air. I didn't understand her anger against me.

Incontinently, I started searching for another job. In May 2013, I got hired at Walgreens working overnight. While working both jobs I was enervated. I decided to relinquish my downtown job. I settled with my overnight job. While working at my new job, I was weary. This was my first time working overnight so I figured that was the cause.

Every night I went to work, I would fall asleep at the register without even knowing. I kept getting warnings from my manager. The constant sleeping had gotten uncontrollable to the point where I just stopped attending. Even after I quit, I was still sleeping my days away. I was always exhausted.

At the end of July 2013, I finally decided to go to the doctor. I was ascertained by my physician that I was 3 ½ months pregnant. I traveled home astonished by the information I had received. Karter, was the man that I was pregnant by. When I wanted to keep my mind unconsciously off my ex-boyfriend Dre, Karter was my run-to guy. He wasn't someone that I examined myself to be with.

I was vulnerable, I only messed with him out of hurt. Although we would talk here and there, it was all prep talk. It only led to one thing only and that was sex. Karter and I, only had a sexual relationship. When I wanted sex, he came and vice versa. There was nothing permanent about what we had other than our puissant eroticism.

Although I didn't care much about who I was pregnant by; I was excited about my pregnancy. I believed that maybe God was giving me another chance, due to me getting an abortion back in January 2011. I had to figure out how was I going to tell Karter. I knew that I couldn't wait too long because he would obviously suspect something. The time approached for me to tell him and I'm not sure why, but I was stunned by his response. The first thing he suggested was an abortion.

"Listen Shamika, I can't have no kids. Find out how much an abortion cost. I will give you the money to go handle that" he said.

"I'm lost, if you can't have any kids than why am I pregnant? I responded sarcastically.

"Shamika, please find out how much it cost so you can hurry up and handle that" he said.

"Karter, if you think I'm going to kill my baby, something is seriously wrong with you. I'm going on 4 months. My baby is pretty much formed, I'd be sick if I did that. I can't believe you would even consider me doing something like that" I said.

"Shamika, why the fuck would you bring a baby into this world that's not wanted?!" he yelled.

"Oh! Now you don't want my baby! I figured that when you spoke up an abortion. I was just waiting on you to say it. Wow Karter! So, you mean to tell me you never wanted a family or baby by me? So, what was all that shit you was talking during sex!" I yelled.

"Cum on Shamika! You know what it was! What the fuck man?! It was sex talk! I was in the moment. Listen I will give you the money to go handle that" he said.

"Karter, I don't want your money. I'm keeping my baby. I thank you for being honest and showing me your true colors. Stay the fuck away from me!" I yelled while hanging up.

When I got off the phone with him, I cried. Karter was right, I knew exactly what it was between me and him. Our sexual relationship was so puissant. I allowed my emotions to get involved. I, then, secluded the reality of this all. I thought about an abortion and I felt nauseous. I thought about how the first abortion made me feel and I just couldn't do it. I still dwelled on the hurt, it still affected me. I tried so hard not to think about it. However, an interruption of chronological sequence took its course willfully.

Flashback:

In January 2011, when I found out I was 12 weeks pregnant, I knew I couldn't keep it. During this time, I lived with my mother who was strict and mean. If she found out I was pregnant she would have put me and my son out. This baby would have been by the man that I was in love with, Dre. I really wanted to keep my baby. However, I couldn't take that risk of being homeless with 2 babies. I immediately got an abortion.

On February 14, 2011, my mother came home angry. I was always her target as usual. She argued with me over 2 dishes that wasn't clean. Now my mother would always come home from work furious. I would always make sure her house was clean and smelling good. I thought that if I did this she would feel relived and not take her frustrations out on me. However, nothing seemed to stop me from being her object of abuse.

This day was different, she wanted those 2 dishes to be cleaned and I refused. My grandma once told me;

"when your mom comes home enraged, just shut your room door and leave her alone."

From the looks of it, this seem to be one of those days. I decided to take my grandmother's advice. I quietly closed my room door while she was in the kitchen yelling.

BOOM! "Don't close no fucking doors in my house! Get in here now and clean my kitchen!" she yelled.

"The kitchen is cleaned" I replied.

"BITCH! You heard what I said!" she yelled.

"What's your problem?! Why are you calling me out my name? I'm not a bitch! you a bitch!" I replied.

"Aw! you wanna be grown! ok, get your shit and get the fuck out my house now!" she yelled.

At that point I was appalled by the disrespectful words that had been exchanged. As my heart raced, I sat on my bed speechless. I was hoping she would just go in her room and calm down.

"What did I say!" she yelled.

"Would you please just leave me alone?" I asked.

"No! the hell with that! You should've thought about that when you called yourself being grown!" she yelled.

From that moment on she started throwing my stuff all everywhere.

"STOP! I will get my own stuff!" I yelled.

She ignored me as she kept pulling and throwing my belongings from my closet. I got up and ran in her living room. I knocked everything down that I possibly could. She charged behind and grabbed me. I was awestruck at how my mother fought me as if I was some stranger off the street. I fought back but I stopped.

"Shamika, what are you doing?" I thought to myself.

She continued fighting me. Grabbing me by my hair, pulling me through the living room and up to the front door. She called my uncle.

"Come get this bitch before I kill her!" she yelled.

I sat there as tears raced down my face. I looked over to my son; David and little sister; Samantha, who was crying uncontrollably. They witnessed everything yet too young to voice what had taken place. While tightly gripping my hair, my mother kept swinging my head and neck around. My neck was in pain, but I had no control.

"You are going to regret this day" I cried.

The police came and was asking what happened. My mother blamed me for everything. Due to her being employed by the City of Chicago, they believed her.

"Get you some clothes and leave now! Are you crazy?! disrespecting your mother! you should be ashamed of yourself!" yelled one of the police officers.

Tears silently streamed in every direction down my face. I tried to grab as much clothes for me and my baby as possible. I had no idea where I was going to go. I was wrong for calling my mother out of her name, however; she was wrong for provoking me. She was wrong for forcing me to encounter whatever it was that tormented her, daily.

Meanwhile, I could hear my mother and the police officers laughing. They begin to conversate about their jobs within the City of Chicago. I felt abandoned and helpless. If my own mother cared nothing for me, who could possibly do so.

Even if my father and mother abandon me, the Lord will hold me close. -Psalms 27:10 NLT

While gathering my clothes, my aunt; Vicky, walked in.

"What happened?" she asked.

I tried to explain however, anxiety took its course and I was unable to.

"It's alright, we will talk some other day. Get you and the baby enough clothes and come with me" she said.

"Ok" I responded.

I stayed with Vicky for the remaining month of February and the whole month of March. I was hurt from what my mother did to me. I didn't allow that to discourage me from doing what I needed to do, though. I had a son to raise. I made a vow to myself that I would never let him see me sweat. I would never be infuriated to the point where I'm making him my target. It wasn't fair, and he should never have to feel the way I felt.

I registered for school full time and worked at a movie theatre part time. On April 12, 2011, I received my first 2- bedroom apartment. I had been on the waitlist for 4 years. This was the perfect timing for me and my baby to finally have our own space. We now had a place that we could call home. I appreciated my aunt for taking me and my son into her wings. However, I knew that I couldn't get comfortable and stay there with her forever. Without hesitation, I picked up my keys to my place and immediately started moving in. Once I got settled in my place, I thought about how I could've kept my baby. If only I had known all of this was going to take place.

Retrieving from Flashback:

Laying in my bed, I wept as I thought about how I could've avoided getting that abortion. I made a promise to God that no matter what I was not getting another abortion. In September 2013, I found out I was having a boy. During this time, David was 5years old. During my pregnancy, he would always say I'm having a boy. He was so excited when he found out he was going to be a big brother. Even though, I was filled with acrimony, I was curious to meet my baby boy.

I was working a part time job while I was pregnant. I was barely surviving but I made it through by the Grace of God. There was not a day that went by, that I didn't think about what my mother did to me. It only bothered me more knowing that I was pregnant by a man who cared nothing for me. I was broken on the inside and furious with everyone whom surrounded me.

At times I wouldn't eat or drink anything. I wanted to, but I never seemed to have an appetite. Everything I ate came right back up. In October 2013, my labor was getting ready to be induced. My baby wasn't due until January 2014. I didn't want to risk him coming any earlier than he was supposed to. Not only was I depressed, I was making my unborn baby suffer as well.

I was admitted to the nearest hospital. It was so bad that I had stay there for 2 days. I hadn't attended church in months. The bible that Mrs. Eternal gave me was somewhere in my apartment collecting dust. I laid in the hospital bed, thinking about the day I got baptized. That was the best day of my life. Somehow, right after I watched as my life fell apart.

"Who was Jesus and why did he allow all of this to happen to me? Whoever he was, he knew me very well. He even shared my information with the Bishop. When I get out of here, I'm going to find out who Jesus really is" I thought to myself.

Chapter Two

The next morning the doctor came in.

"Good morning! I have some great news for you! I will not be inducing your labor and your baby is fine. You were just a bit dehydrated. This created minor contractions, which caused your water bag to leak. I am going to get your discharge papers ready and you will be released today. Be sure to drink lots and lots of water. Also, try to eat small portions of food. Do you have any questions for me?" she asked.

"No" I responded.

"Alright" she said.

I laid in the hospital bed thanking God silently because I knew deep down inside that he had come to my rescue.

Although, I hadn't been to a church in a while, I would always think about Bishop and Mrs. Eternal. Even though Mrs. Eternal gave me her bible in January 2013, I didn't start reading it until November 2013. The first time opening this bible, I was afraid. I didn't know where to begin. I slowly glanced through all the different books wondering what it was about.

I closed the bible and said a small prayer,

"God, can you lead me and choose which book you desire for me to read first. Honestly, I'm not sure what to do or where to start."

I didn't start reading the bible until the following week. The first book that I started reading was the Book of Proverbs. This book was so good that I didn't want to stop reading it. No matter what, I made it my business to read a chapter a day. If I came across any words that I didn't understand, I searched the definition in the dictionary.

Every day, I grew thirsty and hungry for the Word of God. I wasn't quite sure what love was just yet. Based off the way I was digging deep in his Word. I assumed that maybe this was the first step of learning about love. I was at a place in my life where I wanted more of God. I really wanted to get to know him. I tried everything else in my life and nothing ever seemed to work.

"What's the worst that could happen, if I surrendered all to God for a change in my life?" I thought to myself.

I love all who love me. Those who search will surely find me.
- Proverbs 8:17 NLT

After reading the Book of Proverbs, I started reading the Book of Psalms. This book only made me yearn for more of God. This book taught me how to pray, praise and worship God no matter what. Although I had many questions and was amazed by what I was reading, I didn't stop. Reading God's Word kept my mind on nothing but him. Before I knew it, I found myself posting scriptures all over my house and bedroom. I begin to meditate and store his Word deep within my heart. I found myself going to sleep and waking up reading his Word. I felt free in my mind, body and soul. I felt a way that I had never felt before in my life.

On January 13, 2014 at 2:28pm, my baby boy Keith was born. He came out screaming his lungs out, so I knew he was alright. One thing I noticed about him during the 3 days we spent in the hospital, is that he was frowning. I automatically knew that it was because during my whole pregnancy I was angry. It was difficult for me to look at him sometimes. Keith looked just like Karter with some features of me. He was so adorable though, and I loved him so much.

I decided right then and there, that I was giving up what I was struggling with for the sake of my son. I was the reason that he was born angry with a frown on his face. I made a promise to him at only 3 days old, that I would love him no matter what. During the process of Keith's growth, he was very defensive at such an early age. Once again, I blamed myself. Within time I begin to have patience with him. I was very gentle and calm with him.

At times he would look at me as if I was his enemy. However, I ignored it. I would still talk, sing, read and play around with him. I couldn't be angry with him for acting the way he did, he was just a baby. It wasn't his fault that I carried him bitter for 9 months. Anything to see my baby smile more than he frowned, made me feel good on the inside. This experience taught me that not only did my anger affect me, but it affected those around me as well.

As time went on, I continued to read the Word of God. I kept thinking about going back to church.

"That church is just too far south to be catching the bus" I thought to myself.

One night I got up getting ready to make Keith a bottle. I sat in my bed and silently prayed.

"God, I know there has to be a way where I can go to church without leaving my house. I wish there was a way that I could just attend church over the phone or something. I wish that I could have a pastor that I can talk to and comfort me. Can you send me a pastor like that? Can you send me a pastor who will lead me and show me what love is? Can you please?"

Now instead of me seeking God first. I was like the people of Israel in the book of 1 Samuel. I was asking God to send a Pastor who could fill these voids in me that only he could fill up. By doing this, I was rejecting him in many ways. I preferred a Pastor who could lead me astray at any time over God. What I failed to realize is that God is God over everything…No man is greater than him. However, I didn't fully understand what I was asking for.

Scripture from Book of 1 Samuel to better help reader understand author

Finally, all the elders of Israel met at Ramah to discuss the matter with Samuel. "Look," they told him, "you are now old, and your sons are not like you. Give us a king to judge us like all the other nations have." Samuel was displeased with their request and went to the Lord for guidance. "Do everything they say to you," the Lord replied, "for they are rejecting me, not you. They don't want me to be their king any longer. Ever since I brought them from Egypt they have continually abandoned me and followed other gods. And now they are giving you the same treatment. Do as they ask, but solemnly warn them about the way a king will reign over them."
-1 Samuel 8:4-9 NLT

From that day forward, I kept reading and mediating on the Word of God. Even though, I stayed in his Word, there was nights that I couldn't sleep. It would feel like something heavy was on top of me. I couldn't breathe, talk or move. I didn't know what it was, and I wasn't sure if I could talk to God about it. I was still afraid to talk to him at times. I treated God like everyone else, I didn't allow myself to be fully available to him. I told him what I felt he should know and kept the rest to myself. Of course, this didn't do me any justice. For God to fully have his way with me, I had to open my heart completely to him. Instead of me praying about it, I just decided to sleep in the daytime since it only took place at night.

At times I would go to my mother house with my boys and stay there for weeks, just to get some rest. While at her house, I would have to leave after so long. I would think about the pain that she caused me. I always went around her thinking that someday she would apologize. I wanted her to explain to me why she treated me the way she did. However, If I stayed around her for too long, I would start to feel sick to my stomach.

I would get angry and irritated for no reason at all and want to go back home. I would think about why I felt that way, but I could never come up with an answer. For some odd reason, I was afraid to pray about it. I thought that since I didn't know, God didn't know either.

In October 2014, an old friend of mines by the name of Mona, reached out to me. She explained to me that her sister is a Pastor and owns a church. She gave me the dates and times for the upcoming service. I was excited.

"This must be God! It has to be God!" I thought to myself.

Seek his will in all you do, and he will show you which path to take. - Proverbs 3:6 NLT

Now before I went to this service I didn't think to talk to God about it first. To be honest, I was still a baby in Christ. I really didn't know that I had to place God first in everything. When the time arrived for me to attend the first service, I was anxious. I made it there right on time.

Be anxious for nothing, but in everything by prayer and supplication, with thanksgiving, let your request be made known to God; and the peace of God which surpasses all understanding, will guard your hearts and minds through Christ Jesus.
-Philippians 4:6-7 NKJV

It seemed suspicious when I first got there. The lights were dim, and no one was there. Mona, was her sister and she wasn't even there but I didn't care. After waiting awhile, a lady walked out dressed in all black.

"Hey, how are you? I'm Prophetess Winter Blind" she said.

"Hi, I'm Shamika" I responded as we shook hands.

"Now tell me a little about yourself" she said.

"Well I have 2 boys and my own place. I'm searching for a church where I can just stay at home. Due to me losing my car, traveling south is too far to be going to church" I said.

"Wow! Ok, have you been baptized?" she asked.

"Yes, I got baptized in the beginning of 2013. I would really like to get to know God. I've been through a lot and I just want more of him" I responded.

"I can see your pain just by looking into your eyes. How is your relationship with your mother?" she asked.

Instantly, I begin to cry, and I couldn't respond.

"Aww baby girl… I know, I know; it's gone be alright. I can hear your heart, God loves you so much. You are in the right place" she said.

When she hugged me and said these things to me, all I could think about was how good that hug felt. In my mind, I begin to wish my mother could hug me just like this. Soon after, a man walked in.

"Hello!" he said.

"Hey baby, this is Shamika. Shamika, this is my husband Elder Larry Blind" she said.

"Hi" I responded, as I shook his hand.

I begin to feel a bit uncomfortable because no one else was there, neither did anyone else show up.

"Maybe this is how it's supposed to be" I thought to myself.

Elder Blind pulled himself up a chair and set across from us. He stared at me for a while, then he spoke.

"See you want validation but what you need to understand is that we serve a jealous God. Shouldn't nobody be praised and worshipped but him" he said.

I sat there lost because I didn't understand what he was talking about.

"Well these are Pastors that I prayed for, they can't be wrong, maybe he's right about me" I thought to myself.

Dear friends, do not believe everyone who claims to speak by the Spirit. You must test them to see if the spirit they have comes from God. For there are many false prophets in the world.
-1 John 4:1 NLT

Now in this case, I didn't know myself. So, any and everything they said, I figured it was true. Due to them being Pastors, they couldn't be wrong in my eyes. Even though I just met them, I believed they knew me better than I knew myself.

"How is you and your mother relationship?" he asked.

"Wait! Wait! Now we will talk about that later"
Prophetess Blind interrupted.

"Why?... Oh, I see! Your mother hurt you huh?
Now your holding on to the pain and unforgiveness.
Unforgiveness will make you sick, you need to let that go,
or you will suffer" he said.

"Oh, that's what that is...unforgiveness? that's what
I'm feeling towards my mother" I thought to myself.

As they both continue to talk, I sat quietly and
listened to their every word. Right before I left, Prophetess
Blind gave me more information regarding her church
services. She provided me with the numbers, codes and
schedule to join her prayer line. She explained to me that
she's been operating her church over the prayer line for 5
years now. Saturday, October 25, 2014, was the first day
that she decided to start a small service.

Monday-Friday prayer was at 4-4:30am.
Wednesdays bible study was at 7-8pm. Thursdays women's
prayer was at 8-8:30pm. Bi-weekly on Saturdays service
was from 4-5pm. Everything was mainly held over the
prayer line except service on Saturdays.

Every day I was faithfully on the prayer line. I was
so excited because now I had a pastor who could teach me
about God. I made sure I attended service faithfully every
other Saturday. After a couple of months, I realized that I

wasn't the only one a part of this church. There was a married couple who lived in North Carolina, that visited the line daily as well.

Their names were Diana and Terry. There was two other older women from Texas, who joined the prayer line only on Thursday nights, I was unaware of their name. There was also a woman named Tia from Florida, who was apart as well. As time went on, I begin to draw close to Prophetess Blind. I would talk to her more than I talked to God. In my eyes, she was everything I ever needed.

Prophetess Blind was a big woman. She was dark skinned and always wore makeup. She did her own her hair and kept her nails done. She didn't dress up much, she would always wear the same clothes. She didn't have a job, neither did she go outside unless it was something very important she had to do. She had 4 kids, 2 was coming out of high school and 2 were still in grammar school.

Although she stated that she was an MUA consultant, the only face I seen her do makeup on was her own. When she spoke, her voice was puissant and controlling. She would always say,

"After me, God is not sending anyone else to save his people."

I really didn't know what she meant by that, but I felt like I couldn't lose her. I felt that if I ever lost her…my chances with God would be impossible. One day after service, rushing trying to leave out, I called Prophetess Blind by her first name.

"Bye Winter! Bye everyone! see you all next time" I said.

However, no one responded back so I thought no one heard me. The following day Prophetess Blind called me while I was grocery shopping.

"Hey, I have a question for you. What did you call me when you left out of here yesterday?" she asked.

"I called you by your name" I replied.

"Don't you ever call me by my name! You are to call me pastor! I am your pastor! Not your friend or anything else in that matter! Call me Pastor!" she demanded.

"Ok, well I didn't know that I had to call you something specifically other than your name. Now that I know I will call you Pastor" I replied.

"Good! So now we're clear" she said.

"Wow! Where did that come from? All I did was call her by her name" I thought to myself.

As time went on I was still struggling with the situation regarding my mother. Although I hated Karter, I started seeking attention from him. I wanted him to be a part of Keith's life so bad. Every time I turned around, I continuously found myself seeking answers from him. I was trying to figure out what was the reason behind him rejecting our son. I don't think he had a good explanation as to why he did. He would always just blame me for everything.

There would be times I would be thinking about certain things regarding Karter and Prophetess Blind would call me out the blue. We would start off talking about normal things. She, then, would come out and say exactly what I was thinking about. This blew my mind because I never recalled sharing anything with her. This situation regarding Karter stayed on my mind. One day Prophetess Blind called me.

"Hey baby girl, there is something I want to talk to you about. Do you have a minute?" she said

"Hey Pastor, Yes, I do. What's going on? I responded.

"You need to leave that man alone. I can hear God saying you are never going to get the answer you are looking for. Your son is fine, he doesn't need him. God is saying you need to block him. He desires for you to block all avenues so that he don't have any access to you or your son" she said.

"Maybe God is right, lately I've been trying to get through to this man regarding my son. He just doesn't care, I guess I will just block him." I said.

"Good" she replied.

On the following Saturday, when I attended service it was just me and my boys again. Prophetess Blind oldest two kids would come sometimes. Her younger kids were always there. Sometimes her mother and sister would come. On this day, we were all sitting around as Prophetess Blind explained how God was getting ready to call a fast. She explained the different foods that we can and can't eat. This was my first time ever even going a fast.

"I'm not going on the fast. I can't do that, we can't do anything. I would have to limit what I eat and drink! That's impossible, I'm not doing it" I said.

Everyone looked at me and slowly glanced at Prophetess Blind. She didn't say anything, she just looked at me and smiled. The next day, I was out with my mom running errands when Prophetess Blind called me.

"Hello, how are you?" she said.

"Hey, I'm fine and you?" I replied.

"I'm alright. I wanted to talk to you about something, do you have a minute?" she asked.

"Yes. What's going on?" I said.

"Listen, I don't know what you're use to neither do I know how you operate. However, here at this ministry we are not traditional. God has called and chosen me to do a new thing in the earth. When I'm telling you to do something you can't tell me no. Especially when I'm giving instructions specifically from God. If this is not where you want to be, let me know now. If you chose to be elsewhere doing your own thing then go ahead. I don't play when it comes to God and his Word. I chose to serve the Lord and be obedient no matter the cost. So, tell me what do you want to do? Remember after me, God is not sending another Prophet to save his people, that's it!" she said.

"Ok, where is all of this coming from?" I asked.

"It's coming from you telling me NO! regarding the fast. You don't tell the one that God has placed over you, NO!" she said.

"I didn't tell you No, I said that I can't do it. It's too much and I've never been on a fast before. I just don't think I can do it this time" I replied.

"Ok" she said.

That night when I went to sleep, I kept tossing and turning. I dreamed of snakes and spiders trying to get ahold of me. I kept hearing someone call my name but when I got up I didn't see anyone. I kept hearing someone talk about the fast. I couldn't hear clear enough to understand what the person was saying. I hopped up, tormented while sweating… screaming,

"YES! I WILL GO ON THE FAST!"

The next morning, I called Prophetess Blind and told her about the previous night.

"You cannot tell your leader "No". Neither can you refuse to do what your leader tells you to do. I am here to help and lead you. When you refuse, God will deal with you." she said.

From that day forward, I knew to never tell Prophetess Blind, no again. She knew God better than I did and I knew she wouldn't do anything to harm or lead me astray.

Chapter Three

In August 2015, I got an excellent job paying more than
I've ever been paid an hour. It was an overnight position,
but I didn't mind. I was just grateful to be back working
again. Me and Prophetess Blind begin to draw closer and
closer. We talked almost every day and I told her every
little thing about me, and my family. One day she called
me.

"Hey, I need to talk to you about something. I will
discuss it with you when I see you on Saturday" she said.

"Ok, is everything alright?" I replied.

"Yes. Everything is fine. Go on with your day, I
will see you soon" she said.

"Alright" I replied.

When Saturday arrived, after service Prophetess Blind
pulled her chair to the side next to me.

"I am moving to North Carolina. Me and Elder
Blind had planned on leaving sooner but I can't leave you.
The year 2017 before the summer is when God has decided
for us to move. This is the Will of God. I know this will be
something new for you and the boys. I know it will be

different for your family to not have you all around as well. I want you to think about it, do not tell anyone just yet. What are your thoughts?" she said.

Now, I was amazed because a couple of days prior to this one, for some odd reason I started thinking about moving out of town. However, I was looking into moving to Atlanta not North Carolina. It was so strong on me to move though.

"How did she know I was thinking about moving even before I told her my thoughts?" I thought to myself.

Sitting there in deep thought…

"Yes, I will go if you say it's the Will of God. I would do anything to get more of God while being pleasing in his sight" I said.

"Wow! Praise God! Ok, again don't say anything about it because there will be a lot of backlash. I just want you to be strong enough when the time is near" she said.

That night, while I was at work I had a lot on my mind. I was still thinking about what my mother had did to me. I never dreaded the thought about how I had a baby with a man who cares nothing for me or his son.

"Why am I feeling this way? I'm a part of a new church now but I still feel weighed down" I thought to myself.

I decided to call my friend Miya. She was my only friend here in Chicago. I've known her since grammar school, but our friendship grew stronger throughout our high school years. Miya knew all my secrets. She knew me better than anyone else. The only thing about Miya was that deep down inside she didn't trust me. Due to a misunderstanding in our past, I knew her loyalty was no longer with me. Sitting at my work desk, I reminisced on the cause of it all.

Flashback:

In October 2011, I had a girl's night out with Miya and two of my co-workers; Mona and Tiffany. We all went half on a bottle of white Remy, Hennessy and Tropicana orange juice. We decided that we would chill at my place and get white girl wasted. Tiffany rode with Miya and I rode with Mona. We decided to stop at Popeye's to put something on our stomach before we started drinking.

We ordered our food and headed to my place. We all ate first and decided to walk around the neighborhood. While walking I decided to pull out the liquor. I mixed white Remy, Hennessy and orange juice together.

"You know you shouldn't mix dark and light liquor together. I used to do that until the day I got poisoned" said Miya.

"Whatever, how bad could it possibly be?" I said.

"Ok, you gone see. Don't you start acting crazy either, cause ion got time" she said.

"Ain't nobody gone be acting crazy" I laughed.

"Yea ok Shamika…you don't know what I have to deal with when you get drunk. Ion got time to be fighting people for no reason. I just want to have a chill night" she said.

"Ok" I replied.

In my mind I didn't care what she was talking about. All I cared about was getting rid of this pain I kept feeling inside of me. I wanted it to all go away. After walking through a couple of blocks, we all decided to go back to my place. When we made it back in, we went in my room, sat on the floor and started gossiping about other coworkers at work. I felt light-headed as I laughed but I didn't feel that pain anymore. As Mona and Tiffany talked, I stared at Miya.

"Why did you tell your mom and sister about what happened with me and my mom?" I blurted out.

"Shamika please don't start...What are you talking about?" said Miya.

"You know exactly what I'm talking about! Every time I go around your sister she always saying something. She makes comments about me and my mom as if she knows what happened. Does she know what happened? Did you tell her?" I asked.

"No. she doesn't know. I didn't tell her anything. It's just that sometimes she would ask me questions about you and your mom. I would just tell her something for her to stop asking me" she said.

"What do you mean you would just tell her something so that she could stop asking you? That was none of her business! If anybody ever asked me anything about you and your mother relationship, I'm not gone say nothing about your business. I'm gone act like I don't know anything. How could you do this to me? You know how that makes me feel. What my mother did to me hurts so bad" I cried.

Mona and Tiffany quietly listened, as they both observed. They didn't know us by far, we all just worked together. Miya got up in silence and left, Tiffany followed behind because that was her ride back home. Mona stayed with me and watched me as I cried uncontrollably.

"It hurts! It hurts! Oh God! It hurts! Please take it away! My mother doesn't love me and the man I'm in love with doesn't love me! My son isn't his, yet I named him after him anyway! Please take it away! I need to call him... I have to call him and tell him the truth!" I cried.

Not knowing what was going on, Mona comforted me.

"Shamika, Its ok. Just calm down" she said.

Crying and shaking, I picked up my phone and called my first love, Dre.

"Hello" Dre said.

"David is not yours, Kris is his father. I'm so sorry! I love you so much. I just couldn't keep living a lie! It's killing me on the inside. I felt that you needed to know" I cried.

Dre didn't say a thing instead he just hung up the phone. Laying on my bed as I cried, Mona called her oldest sister.

"Winter, can you pray for my friend? We were drinking, and things got out of control" she said.

Mona put her phone on speaker as her sister prayed for me.

Retrieving from Flashback:

I decided to call Miya and get her feedback on everything.

"Hey, you sleep?" I asked.

"Not yet, what's going on?" she said.

"I just don't understand how this man want no parts of his child. All because I decided to keep my baby. This is his actual son and he wants nothing to do with him. This just don't feel good at all, it hurt so bad. I really don't know what to do. I keep trying to talk to him, but he keeps blaming me for everything. The way I see things... it takes two. Regardless of what I decided to do, he needs to be a man and take care of his responsibilities. Every time, I think about this it makes me furious all over again" I explained.

"Shamika, I know it don't feel good. I'm not saying what he is doing is right. However, let's look at the bigger picture here. David don't even know who his real father is because of you, a selfish choice you made. Are you thinking about the hurt you have caused Dre? Are you thinking about the pain that Kris is feeling not being able to see his son?" she said.

"What does Karter and Keith have to do with Dre, Kris, and David?" I asked.

"What do you mean? Do you hear yourself right now? It's the same situation with different people. The only difference is that Karter is Keith real father. Karter is acting selfish and only thinking about himself, no doubt. However, this situation is only giving you a dose of your own medicine. Listen, don't worry about Keith and why Karter is rejecting him. Leave that alone…What you need to be doing is getting in contact with Kris. At least try to make things right for David. Try to fix this first. Do the right thing and later down the line… if it's meant, Karter will come around and do right by Keith" she said.

"You're right, I never looked at it this way. I will reach out to Kris as soon as possible." I replied.

"Ok, well girl I'm finna go to sleep" she said.

During my break at work, I went to my car to take a nap. There was never a night that went pass that I didn't dream of witches, snakes, rats and spiders. I was tired of dreaming like this. Every time I told Prophetess Blind about it, she would say its witchcraft. I never heard of anything like this. I never had witchcraft dreams in my life, they just came from out of nowhere.

The following morning after work, I dropped my boys off to school and headed home for another nap.

Before I went to sleep I laid in my bed thinking about everything Miya said.

"What would Kris say when I reach out to him? It's been 7 years that I've kept our son away from him" I thought to myself.

My phone rung. It was Prophetess Blind, but I didn't answer. Instead I watched her call until she stopped.

"So…you just gone watch me call and not answer the phone" she texted.

"How do she even know that I'm up watching her call" I thought to myself.

I still didn't respond.

In October 2015, I reached out to Kris and apologized for keeping David away from him. He accepted my apology.

"I have been praying for my son for some time now. Thanks for reaching out. Can he spend the weekend with me? Do he need anything?" said Kris.

I was astonished. I wasn't expecting that kind of response so soon.

"Sure, you can get him whenever you like. First, let me explain everything to him so that he would have a better understanding" I responded.

"Ok cool. Whenever he's ready just let me know" he said.

Now, Kris was a cool guy. He was tall and light-skinned. He was mixed with black and Philippian. I was young when I first laid eyes on him. He would always pick me up, take me out and spoil me. He wasn't a bad guy, my heart just wasn't with him, it was with Dre.

I messed with them at the same time. I didn't know what to do once I got pregnant by Kris. I lied and stayed away from him to keep what I had going on with Dre. I never thought the consequences would catch up with me later down the line.

With all this taking place, I was still going to church. Service was now every Sunday from 4-5pm. The year was almost over. I was excited because I was getting ready to move to North Carolina. I begin to draw closer and closer to Prophetess Blind. Every word she preached locked in my memory. I stored numerous notebooks with every word she taught. On Wednesday night during bible study, I remember her saying;

"If everybody is saying the same thing about you, something is wrong. Now if it's one person that's ok. When numerous people are constantly saying the same thing about you or something you're doing, something is definitely wrong."

I was faithful on the prayer line, bible study and attending church. I was enervated, every time I felt this way I blamed my mother and drew closer to Prophetess Blind. I got so attached to her that I told her everything. It got so bad that I started calling to get her permission before I made any decisions. Although I did this every chance I got, I still didn't feel free.

"Who else do I have? Who else can I run to that will listen and love me the way she does" I thought to myself.

As time went on I kept taking notes of everything Prophetess Blind preached. However, she wanted me to post my notes on Facebook.

"Sigh…sometimes I feel like no one is getting the Word of God. Everybody is doing what they want to do. No one is doing it for the sake of this ministry" she said.

"Do you want me to post the notes from bible study on Facebook?" I asked.

"Yes! Please! then maybe others will come once they hear the truth" she responded.

"Ok" I said.

Every Wednesday after bible study I would post the notes on Facebook. Malcolm, my coworker from the theatre I use to work at, started liking every note I posted. Now Malcolm was like me when it came to God. He was a man after God's heart and would do anything according to God's Will. Malcolm had a big family and they always did things together, they were very close. Malcolm's mother was a praying woman of God. She never missed a day of church and she always prayed for all her children.

Malcolm was baptized and raised in the church that I got baptized in. Malcolm just wanted to be pleasing in the sight of the Lord. He would do anything if it was the Will of God. After posting so many notes, Malcolm inbox me on Facebook.

"Hey, Shamika! That's some powerful stuff you be posting on here. What church do you go to? I would like to attend sometimes" he said.

"Sure, no problem. Give me one second" I replied.

I had to make sure it was ok with Prophetess Blind first before I gave anyone her number or address. When she agreed to everything, I gave Malcolm her information. From that day forward, Malcom started getting on the prayer line and attending service. His girlfriend, Anna came along with him. So now it wasn't only me that was a part of this ministry. It was Malcolm, Anna, Tia, Diana, Terry and Diana two friends; China and Valerie.

A little bit after China joined she was no longer apart of the ministry. I noticed after a while I didn't hear her praying on the prayer line anymore. I asked Prophetess Blind about it.

"Hey, is everything alright?" I asked.

"Yes, why do you ask that?" she said.

"I just don't hear China on the line anymore" I said.

"Oh, honey! That's because she thinks that I'm supposed to run my ministry like the church she once attended. I kept trying to tell her this ministry is not traditional. God is doing a new thing in the earth. She didn't want to be obedient, so God told me rebuke and release her" she explained.

"Wow! That was quick" I said.

"Yes, it was baby girl. I must obey God when he gives me specific instructions. If people refuse to listen, they will be rebuked and released.

The next day I got up excited. The move to North Carolina was approaching fast. Immediately, I started thinking about how it would be when we all move.

"With all the money saved up from the tithes and offerings we are going to be able to get a big church. People will come and be saved" I thought to myself.

While thinking about this my phone rung, it was Prophetess Blind.

"Hey, what are you doing?" she asked.

"Nothing, I woke up feeling good today. What about you? how are you?" I said.

"I'm alright, I was just checking on you" she said.

After having a small conversation before hanging up, I realized she knew exactly what was on my mind again without me telling her.

"Do you have your bible in front of you? I want to go over something with you really quick" she said.

"Yes, I do" I responded.

"Ok. Turn to *1 Corinthians 9:16-18 NLT*

"one second... Ok, I'm there" I said.

"It reads: *Yet preaching the Good News is not something I can boast about. I am compelled by God to do it. How terrible for me if I didn't preach the Good News! If I were doing this on my own initiative, I would deserve payment. But I have no choice, for God has given me this sacred trust. What then is my pay? It is the opportunity to preach the Good News without charging anyone. That's why I never demand my rights when I preach the Good News.*

So, you see I can't get mad when people don't pay their tithes and offerings. I preach the Word of God because this is what God called me to do. Now, if this was me doing my own thing then I would get angry. However, I can't because I wouldn't really be doing God's Will. Do you understand?" she said.

"Yes" I responded.

"Ok, well I don't want to hold you for long. Go ahead and enjoy your day baby girl" she said.

"Ok" I responded.

Although I stated I understood what she was saying, I really didn't know what she was talking about. I was thinking about all the tithes and offerings that was saved for the new church, I assumed would be built in North Carolina. I'm not sure why I thought about this. Something in me believed that the tithes and offerings should be used specifically to build the church. I was confused but I didn't think anything of it.

Should people cheat God? Yet you have cheated me! "But you ask, "What do you mean? When did we ever cheat you?' "You have cheated me of the tithes and offerings due to me. You are under a curse, for your whole nation has been cheating me. Bring all the tithes into the storehouse so there will be enough food in my temple. If you do," says the Lord of Heaven's Armies, "I will pour out a blessing so great you won't have enough room to take it in! Try it! Put me to the test! – Malachi 3:8-10 NLT

After a while the consistency on the prayer line was getting worse. At times it would just be me and Prophetess Blind on the line. I could hear the frustration in her voice as she prayed. The more we all prayed I noticed that I didn't hear Valerie on the prayer line anymore. One morning when I got off work, Prophetess Blind called me.

"Someone tried to break into my PayPal account!" she yelled.

"What do you mean?" I asked.

"I think it was Valerie because it says that it took place in Washington, DC. She is the only one from Washington that's a part of this ministry" she said.

"Why would she try to break into your account?" I asked.

"I'm not sure. We did have a conversation about tithing. She kept promising me that she would pay a large amount of money. When she got the money she never gave unto the Lord" she explained.

"How do you know she have any money?" I asked.

"Well lately she has been flashing it all over Facebook. She's been out taking her daughter on shopping sprees but haven't paid her tithes. This is why people don't have nothing because they refuse to pay their tithes unto the lord first. I can see it now God is getting ready to release her but I'm going to wait and see. God will deal with her" she said.

"That's not right that she is doing this to you. I don't understand why people are constantly treating you this way. First China and now Valerie, this is crazy. It's unfair" I replied.

"Well, baby girl people get crazy over their money. No, it's not right but that's how folks are. Go on with your day, I will talk to you soon" she said.

"Ok" I responded.

When I got off the phone, I tried to understand why would Valerie do such a thing? Prophetess Blind only wants to help people draw closer to God.

"Why is Prophetess Blind monitoring Valerie's money and keeping tabs on her tithings? Well maybe…naw we already discussed that she doesn't preach the Word of God to get paid so that can't be it. I don't know what's going on" I thought to myself.

Later that day I went to pick up my boys from school. I ran into Mrs. Eternal.

"Praise God! How are you?" she said.

I smiled because it felt so good to see her.

"Hey, I'm alright! How have you been?" I said.

"Oh, I am blessed! I haven't seen you at church in a while. Are you going to church elsewhere?" she asked.

"Yes, I'm a part of a small church held inside of a house. I've been there for a while now and I like it. I have never been so close to God in my life." I said.

"Praise God! But wait now you say it's in a house, are you sure it's a church? I ask because sometimes you must be careful. People will come off like its God but it's not. Don't worry though because if it's not God he will keep you and show you" she said.

"Ok" I responded.

Now lately my family seemed suspicious and they barely talked to me. My mother would always say,

"Shamika that lady is a witch! She's using you to pay her bills in that house! She's not right!"

My mother always had something negative to say when it came to me, so I didn't listen to her. Every time we talked if she said something negative about my church or my pastor, I ended the conversation quick. She never wanted to see me happy. It was always something with her and I was always her target. The only one in my family that I stayed in contact with was my cousin Faith.

Faith would always call me from time to time and check on me. She never pressured me about the church I went to. If she did feel the same way as my mother, I would've never known it. Every time I talked to her we had a normal conversation. I knew that I could talk to Faith about anything, yet I was still a bit skeptical. I didn't want her to eventually start judging me like everyone else.

As time went on, the move to North Carolina proceeded quick. Before I knew it, Valerie was no longer apart of the ministry. Prophetess Blind would call me almost every day. She started to complain a lot about Tia. Tia would get on the prayer line whenever she could make it on. She was married to a man in the military. Whenever her husband traveled she went along with him. Her husband's next move was to Italy. Prophetess Blind explained to her that she need to be with us headed to North Carolina.

"Folk just want to do what they want to do. I keep trying to tell the people of God that God is not sending another prophet after me. Once I'm gone, I'm gone there is no turning back. That's it!" she said.

At times just hearing her talk I would be afraid to speak my mind about certain issues. I didn't want God to be angry with me. She would always call me and talk about everyone in the ministry. She would always say,

"I don't want you to think I'm gossiping because I'm not, I am just venting."

I trusted her, I knew she didn't mean any harm to anyone. I would just be quiet and listen to every word she spoke. She would go on and on about Malcolm, Anna, Diana, Tia, and Terry. It's like everything they did bothered her.
Malcolm and Anna had been together for 8 years. I'm not sure how their relationship was but they were a beautiful couple in my eyes. They liked to hang out and maybe even have a drink every now and then. I'm not sure how Anna relationship was with her family because I always seen her with Malcolm's family. Anna had her own way of dressing. She knew how to do hair and makeup very well. Anna was amazing and talented to me.
One morning, Prophetess Blind called me.

"Good morning, you busy?" she said.

"Good morning, no I'm not busy what's going on?" I responded.

"I'm just tired, sometimes I feel like I'm doing something wrong or maybe I'm not saying the right things" she said.

"I think you're doing very well at everything. Why do you feel this way? Is everything alright?" I asked.

"I just feel like when people join my ministry they should be delivered. People are not going to come to my ministry and do as they please. I refuse to see them walk out of here the same way they came in" she said.

"Well, what do you mean by that?" I asked.

"Malcolm and Anna are having sex and they are not married. Malcolm was just on Facebook holding a cup of liquor in his hands while praying to God. However, he says he wants more of God. Anna, is always dressing half naked and she thinks it's cute. She is going to constantly attract the wrong attention. All of this is just displeasing in the sight of the Lord. If it's not right to God, it doesn't sit right with me neither" she explained.

"Ok. Well maybe you should talk to them about it. Let them know that what they are doing is not right" I said.

"I did but they are still doing it as if I didn't say anything. I am going to have to sit down with them and talk about it again. This is unacceptable" she said.

Every Sunday after service, I noticed that Malcolm, Anna, Prophetess and Elder Blind would be talking about marriage.

"So how long y'all been together?" asked Elder Blind.

"It's been 8 years now" said Malcolm.

"So, what's the hold up? What is it? Are you scared?" asked Elder Blind.

"To be honest, I'm not sure, I wouldn't say I'm scared though" Malcolm replied.

"If you don't want to get married, don't do it but this is not pleasing in the sight of the lord. Especially since you say you're a man of God. Marriage is not what everyone makes its seem to be but see I had to do what was right" said Elder Blind.

"Definitely! Definitely! I will look into it."
Malcolm replied.

"What's there to look into? You say this is the
woman that you love right? You been with her for 8 years
now, how much more time do you need to be sure?" asked
Elder Blind.

"Yeah, you right. No doubt" laughed Malcolm.

Malcolm and Anna were a beautiful couple. I just don't
think Malcolm was ready for marriage. Ready or not, I
thought he was supposed to make that choice without being
forced. As Malcolm and Elder Blind continued talking. I
watched as Prophetess Blind set aside and observed.
        It was like this was all a part of her plan or
something. I didn't know much about God. However, I'm
sure if Anna was chosen to be Malcolm's wife, it wouldn't
have taken 8years for him to realize this. It wouldn't have
taken Elder Blind to present marriage and force it on him
either.

"How about we set up marriage counseling? You
both think about it and let me know what's best for you"
said Prophetess Blind.

"Ok cool" said Malcolm.

Before I knew it; Saturday, November 19, 2016 was the date set for Malcolm and Anna to get married. One morning when I got off work, I received an email from Prophetess Blind. I opened it and glanced over it. However, I was too tired to read it. After a nap, I woke up to a missed call from her. I called her back to see if everything was alright.

"Hey, you alright?" I asked.

"Yes, I'm alright. I called to see if you received the article that I emailed you this morning" she said.

"Yes. I received it, I didn't fully read it though. What is it about?" I said.

"Go ahead and read it, call me back when you're done. I will be able to better explain it to you" she said.

"Ok." I replied.

After getting off the phone with her, I was still so exhausted even after getting some rest. I opened the email and started reading over it. It was an article that talked about King David being King Saul armorbearer. It also talked about King Saul son, Jonathan. It explained how his armorbearer was faithful to him no matter what. It had a lot of scriptures from the book of 1 Samuel. It provided a clear understanding regarding the responsibilities of an armorbearer.

After reading this article, I called Prophetess Blind back.

"Ok, I'm finished reading" I said.

"Wow! That was quick. Ok so tell me your thoughts" she said.

"It's pretty interesting, however, an armorbearer has a lot of responsibilities" I said.

"It's not as bad as you think it might be. It does take a lot of responsibility though. So, just reading over it do you think it's something you would be able to do?" she said.

"what do you mean?" I asked.

"Well, I'm asking because God has called you to be my armorbearer. He showed me this awhile back, but I wasn't sure. Then you started operating in a armorbearer spirit, so I was like ok she's ready. When my husband said it, I really knew then. When he says something, 90 percent of the time he is right. So, tell me what's your thoughts" she said.

"I'm not sure. However, if God has called me to be an armorbearer, then I'm sure that's what I am. God would never lead me astray. When he says something, he is never wrong. So, I'm with it only if it's his Will" I said.

"Wow! You are truly after God's heart. You know lately Tia hasn't been consistent in coming on the prayer line. I honestly don't believe she is coming with us to North Carolina. She is my armorbearer as of now but you're next in line. If she wants to go with her husband to Italy instead of doing the Will of God, that's on her. God will deal with her. She acts like she can't come and be away from her husband for a while. He's barely home anyway due to him being in the military. She hasn't been paying her tithes and offerings. Every time I ask her about it she keeps saying her husband haven't given her any money yet. However, she's always talking about how she just brought this and that" She explained.

"Wow! Well maybe she doesn't have it" I said.

"Really Shamika?! Her husband is in the military. He has it, he just doesn't want to give it. I already know the time is near. God is getting ready to release her from this ministry and its nothing that I can do. I keep trying to tell her that God is not sending anyone else after me, I guess she doesn't care. People want to do what they wanna do. When things get out of hand, they want to call me for prayer. I have no other choice but to pray for them" she said.

Listening to Prophetess Blind I did understand her frustration. One thing I didn't understand though was how she expected Tia to be away from her husband. I'm not sure what it was like being married. However, I know that if Elder Blind had to leave, she'd be right with him. If not, she'd really be throwing tantrums and complaining.

Another thing I didn't understand was her complaining about tithing. She basically made it clear that she works unto the Lord because it's his Will. Not for her own reasons. It's just starting to seem like she is saying one thing yet doing another. I'm not sure if she realizes it but I do.

"Am I the only one who is doing right? Do she vent about me like this to others as well?" I thought to myself.

"Well I don't want to hold you long. I'm just venting. Make sure you pray about being my armorbearer. I just want God to show you for himself" she said.

"Ok." I replied.

After getting off the phone, I realized that I had more time to take me another nap. While I was asleep I had two different dreams. First, I dreamed of me going into this house, but spiders and webs were everywhere. Although they surrounded me, they did not touch me. I was able to get around them.

Once I entered the house I had to go up some stairs. At the top of the stairs there were more spiders. They were huge. Instead the web there were big leeches slowly moving around. One of the leeches got on me but I immediately knock it off, then I woke up.

I stayed up for a little while then I went back to sleep. I instantly went into the second dream. I saw the article regarding the armorbearer. I heard Prophetess Blind voice teaching me as a book flipped pages in front of me. I woke up sweating, feeling like I never went to sleep all over again.

"I guess that was confirmation from God calling me to be an armorbearer" I thought to myself.

The following Sunday I was at service early waiting to hear the Word of God. I noticed that Prophetess Blind made little money packets for us to put our tithes and offerings in. Now, I normally paid my tithes and offerings every other Friday, the day I got paid. As crazy as it may sound, by that Sunday I was broke. Prophetess Blind would be very aggravated when no one gave at service.

"Listen you all need to at least give something when you come to service, a dollar or something" she said.

I felt bad when she said this because I didn't have anything to give. I wasn't only paying tithes and offerings. She insisted that I sow a seed as well every time I got paid. I was also giving her 10 percent of my food stamps. I was all burned out when Sundays came around. I barely had enough money to buy gas to get back and forth to work.

When my payday was near, she would always call me complaining. She would stress how she didn't have this and that for her house. Every time I looked up something was wrong with her stove, refrigerator or her car. For some odd reason, I always felt guilty. I felt like it was my responsibility to take on her burdens.

One night during bible study, Prophetess Blind preached a sermon regarding honoring the one God has called to lead. After bible study I had a talk with her.

"I desire to have more of God. If there is anything you need, let me know. I don't want you to be stressing and worrying about anything. I need your focus to be on God so that I can receive more of him" I said.

"Wow! Alright" she responded.

I really didn't know what I was saying. I just wanted more of God. I figured that if her attention was elsewhere, I wouldn't get to know God. From that day forward, my payday came and went immediately. She would call with a story regarding more money to be given. One day she called me.

"Good morning, you busy?" she said.

"Good morning, No I'm not is everything alright." I asked.

"I'm not sure if I told you but this ministry has a clothes drive. If there is anything that you don't need, feel free to bring it here. I will give it to those who are less fortunate" she said.

"Ok perfect! Thanks for letting me know because I have a lot of things I need to get rid of" I said.

"No problem. Have God spoken to you regarding being my armorbearer?" she asked.

"Yes, he did" I responded.

"Ok. Next Sunday, I need you to come a bit early because we are going to start training. Do you prefer coming before service or do you want to stay after service?" she said.

"I will come before service. Is 2pm alright?" I asked.

"Yes, that fine. I will see you then" she said.

From that day forward, I was training to become her armorbearer. I was also giving up everything in my house. Whether I needed it or not, I would still give it up. It got so bad that I started giving away my baby's clothes, tv, and game system. It was still in pristine condition, nothing was wrong with any of it. I would come home yet my house didn't feel like a home.

I wasn't at peace and I rarely slept at night or in the day. I was constantly having dreams of snakes, rats, wolves, spiders and leeches. I didn't know why all of this kept happening to me. I wondered where it came from, I dreamed of it every day and night.

I was now attending Prophetess Blind house every Sunday at 2pm for training. I stayed afterwards for service as well. During training, Prophetess Blind would always talk about Diana and Terry. She talked about them so bad. I wondered why God hadn't rebuked and released them as fast as he did others.

"I am so glad that you weren't hurt at the church you were baptized at. You are doing what you're supposed to do. At times it's hard for me to get through to Diana and Terry. They've been hurt by their last pastor. Their last pastor practiced witchcraft and treated them like trash.

Diana's mom practice witchcraft as well. She hasn't
been around her mom for years now because of it. I am
her spiritual mother and Elder Blind is her spiritual
father. She has been with me for years now. She still has
some ways that's not right towards me and I know what
it is. She has a disrespectful mouth. She puts more effort
in her work, school and family then she does this
ministry. I keep trying to explain to her that God comes
first. She always expresses that she knows, however, she
doesn't act like it. I can't give up on her though I am all
that she has" she explained.

I sat there quiet as I listened to every word she
spoke. I noticed that her kids were wearing the clothes
and shoes that I had given for the clothes drive. They
were even playing my kids game system. When I saw
this, she immediately began to explain to me why they
were wearing the clothes and playing the game.

"Some of the things you gave the ministry, I
gave to my kids because their clothes and shoes are
getting too small. The rest of the things are put up in the
basement so that we can give it to those that are less
fortunate" she said.

Everything I gave for the clothes drive her kids were
wearing and using. I really didn't know what could've been
put up in the basement. I didn't think anything of it though.
I kept giving everything in my house away.

Back at home, I lived next door to a woman named Linda. She was the sweetest person I knew. If there was anything I needed, she would always make sure I had it.

"You are just the sweetest person I know. You're a very beautiful young woman. I notice you always just stay to yourself and baby that's the way to be around here" she said.

I smiled, "Thank You" I said.

"If it's anything I can do for you and your babies, don't hesitate to ask me" she said.

"Ok. Thank You" I said.

Every so often, I would ask Linda for help. She kept her word and she always came through for me. She rarely asked me for anything. One day, on my off day, I asked Linda to do my hair. She wasn't a beautician, but she knew how to do hair very well.

"Hey Linda, if you're not too busy can you do my hair today?" I asked.

"Sure baby! How do you want me to do it?" she asked.

"I want something big. Something like the bob Marley hairstyle. Can you do that for me?" I said.

"I sure can. Ok, all you need to do is buy the hair you want. I am ready when you are" she said.

"Ok, how much will you charge me for this style?" I asked.

"Baby don't worry about it, I will do your hair for free. All you need to do is buy the hair" she said.

"Oh wow! Thank you so much! Ok, I'll be right back" I said.

Linda did my hair so pretty that night. I looked amazing. I was really feeling myself due to me not doing anything for myself in a long time. I took numerous pictures and posted them on Facebook. Sunday came around and I was headed to service feeling and looking good.

After service, I decided to stay with Prophetess Blind since I didn't have to work that night.

"So, I have a question for you?" said Prophetess Blind.

"Ok, what is it?" I said.

"Yesterday when you posted those pictures talking about your neighbor, were you throwing shade at me?" she asked.

I was stunned that she asked me that. Now a while back I asked Prophetess Blind to do my hair. Her prices were as high as a hair salon. Of course, I was broke, so I decided to wait until I had some extra money. I really wanted to get my hair done. Linda didn't charge me anything, so I went for it. Now when I posted my pictures on Facebook and thanked my neighbor, Prophetess Blind felt some type of way.

"No, I was not throwing shade and I'm sorry if you felt that I was. I was just thanking my neighbor for being so nice and taking the time out to do my hair" I responded.

"Aw ok, I'm just making sure. So, tell me about this neighbor of yours" she said.

"Linda is a really nice woman. There are times when I can really use her help. We help each other when needed" I said.

"Um. Ok, well just be careful" she said.

I didn't understand why she said be careful. I didn't tell her anything bad about my neighbor. After talking about

Linda, we talked a little bit more then I left. That night, I had a dream that I walked in my living room and Linda was sitting in the middle of the floor.

"Can I spend the night?" she asked.

I kept thinking about how she got in my house.

"Yes, you can stay the night" I said.

I went in my room and went back to sleep. The next day I got up, Linda was gone. She didn't say a word, she just left. She took everything in my house with her. I woke up sweating, ran in my living room and turned on all the lights, then I realized it was just a dream. I sat down on my couch and started crying,

"Jesus! What is going on with me? What is all these dreams about? God! I'm so sleepy but I can't sleep! I keep asking my pastor, but she keeps saying its witchcraft. Father, Please! Tell me…show me! What is going on with me? What is witchcraft and why am I just now dreaming of it? Jesus! I'm tired! Please help me! Is this how its suppose to feel walking with you? I'm steady doing right and reading your word but I still feel depleted. I just want to feel the way I felt when you first came and got me. You know that feeling, I felt before I got baptized. It was so comforting, and everything was alright. Please help me!" I prayed.

After praying, I went back to sleep. It had to be God that consoled me that night because I slept so well. I woke up the next morning to numerous missed calls from Prophetess Blind. Still in bed, I called her back.

"Good morning, are you alright?" she said.

"Yes, I'm fine" I said.

Normally I would tell her everything, but I didn't tell her how I cried out to God. I did tell her the dream I had about Linda.

"Ok, that's good. You were on my mind last night, but I know you were sleeping so I didn't call" she said.

"I had another crazy dream, this time about Linda" I said.

"Really! What was it about?" she asked.

"I woke up and she was in my house. She asked me can she spend the night and I agreed. I believe she took all my stuff because when she left, my house was empty" I said.

"See, that's why I told you to be careful. I knew it but see you needed to see for yourself" she said.

"See what?" I asked.

"Shamika, your neighbor is using you. Her motives are wrong when it comes to you. She only helps you so that you can help her in return. She is leeching off you. You need to leave her alone. Do not ask her for anything else and don't give her anything. You must be careful where you are sowing seeds at because you will end up reaping what you sow. She is not right, Um! Um! Leave that alone" she said.

I listened as she spoke while tears silently fell from my eyes.

"Linda is an amazing woman, I just don't understand why I can't talk to her anymore. How can she possibly be using me when a majority of the time I am the one always asking for her help. She has never done any harm to me or my babies. She has always been there in times of need" I thought to myself.

"You there?" she asked.

"Yes, I'm here. I'm just listening" I said.

"I know it hurts baby girl but that's how people are. You gone be alright, go ahead with your day. I will talk to you later" she said.

I rolled over in my bed, laid flat on my back and silently cried.

"Jesus! My neighbor has done no harm to me, why do I have to leave her alone? I don't have my family, or my mother… now my neighbor. I don't have anybody but my pastor. I know she would never lead me astray, she would never lie to me. She is so powerful they way she teaches me your Word. I never heard anyone teach the way she does. Father God, if something is not right please show me, open my eyes and allow me to have your perception. Jesus, help me please! All I want is more of you! All I desire is to be more like you and pleasing in your sight. Why do I feel so drained? Am I not doing your Will? I just don't understand. I can't sleep and I'm constantly dreaming about rats, snakes, spiders, webs and leeches. I keep praying but it's like it gets worse.
Jesus, all I ask is that you help and lead me. Not my Will or anyone else Will oh Lord but let your Will be done" I prayed.

That night while at work, I was reading the book of Psalms. I ran across a scripture that spoke exactly what I was feeling.

In panic I cried out, "I am cut off from the Lord!" But you heard my cry for mercy and answered my call for help.
-Psalms 31:22 NLT.

"Thank You Jesus!" I shouted.

Chapter Four

Sunday morning came around and I was up early getting ready for armorbearer training. I always made it to training on time. If I was running late, I made sure Prophetess Blind knew in advance. When I arrived, we started training as soon as possible.

"I remember I use to go to this church with this woman who was not right. A while after the church permanently closed, a new church she joined reached out to me. The church offered me a large amount of money. They wanted me to pray over her so that she can become a Prophet. God had already shown me that she wasn't a Prophet. He told me not to go and so I didn't show up. This woman is your cousin" said Prophetess Blind.

Now as I was listening to every word she spoke, I got confused when she said my cousin.

"My cousin?!" I shouted.

"Umm hmm! Your cousin" she said.

"Which one?" I asked.

"Sincere" she replied.

Now Sincere was my second cousin. She was a very sweet woman. She meant no harm to anyone. When I was young I would always go to her house with my other cousins. I would always go to church with them as well. Sincere had 4 boys and 1 girl. They all were so silly and fun to be around. I just couldn't believe that Prophetess Blind said that Sincere wasn't a real Prophet.

"So, if she's not a real Prophet then what is she?" I asked.

"I don't know. That's the same thing I was trying to figure out" she laughed.

"Well did you ask God about it?" I asked.

"No, I just left it alone" she said.

Now out of everything that Prophetess Blind ever said, I found that so hard to believe. I had known Sincere basically all my life. She has never come off fake or mean to me. She was a sweet woman who loved the Lord. At that point I sat there and just listened as Prophetess Blind kept talking.

"As an armorbearer we don't fight physically like they did when Saul was the King. We fight in the spirit. We still need to put on the armor of God so that we can be ready always. We are never supposed fight physically only spiritually" she explained.

~ 76 ~

"Do you have any questions?" she asked.

"No, I'm just listening and taking notes" I replied.

"Good, because I want you to always remember this. When someone attacks you verbally or physically. Take it to God and fight spiritually as an armorbearer should" she said.

After training and service, I sat in my car with my boys. I sat there thinking about Sincere.

"If she is not a Prophet, then who is she?" I thought to myself.

While I was thinking to myself David asked me a question.

"Ma, Does the pastor work? I just never seen her go to work or even talk about a job. How does she pay her bills?" he asked.

"I don't know! that ain't none of my business and neither is it yours! You need to stay in a child's place!" I yelled.

"I'm sorry, Ma. I just wanted to know" he said.

The whole ride home, there was silence in the car. Once I made it home, I showered and prepared myself for bed. Laying down, I thought about what my son asked me in the car. I couldn't believe I reacted that way towards him. Me and David had a beautiful bond. If there was anything he wanted to talk about, he felt comfortable enough to share it with me.

There was never a day that went by, where we didn't communicate. I never wanted him to feel how I felt with my mother. When I wanted to talk, she never listened. I felt abandoned and neglected all my life. I knew how that felt and I never wanted my boys to feel that way.

"Jesus, all he did was ask me a question. What is wrong with me?! Why am I so angry and frustrated?! I didn't mean to respond to my baby like that" I prayed.

The next morning, I was headed to drop my babies off to school. Before David went inside, I pulled him to the side.

"I'm sorry about how I responded to you last night. I'm not sure why I did it, but I promise it won't happen again" I said.

"It's alright Ma. I know you didn't mean it. I love you" he said.

"Ok, I love you too! Have a good day at school" I said.

When I returned to my car, I had numerous missed calls from Prophetess Blind. I decided not to call her back until I got home. When I arrived at home, getting ready to take a nap. My phone rung and it was her. Now normally I would be quick to answer the phone but this time I sat there and watched her call.

For some reason, I slowly started feeling weird about her. Instead of taking a nap, I decided to go and do my laundry. While at the laundromat, Prophetess Blind called again, this time I answered.

"Hello, are you alright?" she asked.

"Yes, I'm fine. What's going on" I said.

"Nothing, have you talked to your mother lately?" she asked.

"No, she always got something negative to say. I don't have time for that" I said.

"Well, what is it that she be saying?" she asked.

"She's always calling you a witch and I don't understand why. Are you a witch?" I said.

"I get that a lot" she laughed.

"Are you a witch?" I asked again.

"Girl No!" she said.

"Listen, I called to tell you a good friend of mines invited me to speak at a women's conference. Since you are my armorbearer you need to be there. It will be Saturday, November 12, 2016 at 9am" she said.

"Ok, I will request that day off" I said.

"Yes, make sure you do that. Also, Malcolm and Anna's wedding will be the following Saturday, November 19, 2016 at 4pm. So, see if you can switch shifts or request that day off as well" she said.

"Ok, wow that was quick! So, they decided to get married huh?" I replied.

"I don't play that! Here at this ministry, people will be saved and delivered. There is no in and out. If people want to do as they please, they can but not in my ministry" she said.

"I thought she said I was next in line to be her armorbearer. I'm still training, I'm not sure what to do when I go to this conference with her. I can't believe Malcolm and Anna are getting married. That was so quick! I thought you were supposed to get engaged first and then plan the wedding. Well, I guess that's how it's supposed to be, I don't know" I thought to myself.

When I went back to work, I made sure I requested November 12th off. I was also able to switch shifts for November 19th. Now every year at my job they would celebrate their anniversary for being in business so long. This year, everyone voted to celebrate at Whirly Ball. I was excited, and I looked forward to attending. Whirly Ball was a cool place for adults and kids.

They have many different activities to choose from. You don't necessarily have to be with anyone to enjoy yourself. Although it was only September, I had to put in my request if I was going to attend. My job anniversary celebration was always held right after Thanksgiving. On my break I decided to call Prophetess Blind. I wanted to share this news with her.

"Hey, you busy?" I said.

"Hey baby girl! No, I'm not. What's going on?" she said.

"So, I received some exciting news and I wanted to share it with you" I said.

"Ok, what is it? She asked.

"Ok, so my job is celebrating their anniversary at the end of November. It's free of charge and I can bring someone with me as well" I said.

"Shamika, what does the bible say?" she asked.

"What do you mean?" I asked.

"The bible says; bad company, corrupts what? Good character...right?" she said.

"Yes" I replied.

"Girl you know you are something else with this voice of yours. One minute you're all excited and the next you're sad" she laughed.

"I don't really talk to anyone at my job, I stay to myself. I just wanted to go to enjoy myself. I always wanted to go to this place" I said.

"I understand, but the people at your job are not like you. They are not seeking the Lord and you don't need to be around them. They are going to be smoking, drinking and doing things that you don't do" she said.

You may think you can condemn such people, but you are just as bad, and you have no excuse! When you say they are wicked and should be punished, you are only condemning yourself, for you who judge others do these very same things.
-Romans 2:1 NLT

"But I am not going to be around or with them. I mean it's free. I just wanted to enjoy myself. Just because they choose to do certain things, doesn't mean that I'm going to do them" I said.

"Shamika, I am just trying to help you. You would be disobeying the word of God if you went. If you really want to go, then go. Do what you want to do" she said.

"Ok, my break is almost over. I will talk to you later" I said.

After getting off the phone with her, I was tousled.

"What did anyone else doings have to do with me? I just wanted to go out and have fun. It's not like I was going to be sitting around in everybody face" I thought to myself.

The rest of the day at work I sat quietly at my work desk. My co-worker talked about how much fun it was going to be at Whirly Ball.

"Every event this place have is always fun. Everybody be so laidback while enjoying themselves. It's not any drama or none of that. Sometimes I barely see my managers and coworkers. One thing about this job that I can say is they always make sure we have an enjoyable time," said my coworker.

Listening to my coworker talk, I didn't intervene. I really wanted to go but I didn't want God to be angry with me. I didn't want to find myself doing anything that was displeasing in his sight. By the end of my shift, I decided not to go to the event. I decided to work a double on that day instead. September 16, 2016, Ellis; Karter's mother, reached out to me over Facebook. She commented on a random status of mines.

"I would love to be a part of Keith life if that's alright with you. Too much time has been wasted, please let me know your thoughts"

"What in the world is going on?" I thought to myself.

Now back Keith was three months old, I prayed to God asking if he could someday meet his grandmother on his father side.

"Father God, I know that his father cares nothing for him. That doesn't mean his family feels the same way. Father, if it's of your Will, all I ask is that you allow Keith to someday meet his grandma and build a bond that can never be broken. All I ask is that you allow my baby boy to meet his family on his father's side. Not on my time but on your time Lord" I prayed.

<u>***Thinking back to how it all started***</u>

Keith was now 2 years old. Before his grandmother reached out, I had numerous dreams within the years of her calling me. She would set dates up to meet with me. I also had dreams that I would take him to her house. She would take him out of my hands, embraced him and introduced him to his family.

I never shared these dreams with anyone. During Keith newborn stages, I desired for it to happen; however, it didn't. I would always ask Karter questions about his mother. This didn't help at all, we always ended up arguing.

"What type of person is your mother?" I asked.

"She's a strong and sweet woman. She raised me, my brother and sisters on her own. She didn't depend on child support" he said sarcastically.

"Aw ok…well too bad for her because I depend on it" I laughed.

Every time I talked to Karter, he would always bring up the fact that I put him on child support. Karter was handsome. He was dark skinned, short and cocky. He looked like

Omar Epps with a beard like Rick Ross. He was always in the streets of Chicago and he always did his own thing.

He called the shots when it came to the streets and the woman he messed with. I was different and too much for him to handle. One thing we did have in common was calling the shots. When he tried to tell me what to do and how to do it, that didn't sit well with me. Before Keith was born, Karter would always make promises he had no intentions on keeping.

"Listen, it's a lot going on right now. Just give me some time. If I don't step up and take care of my son, then put me on child support" he said.

"Whatever Karter ain't shit going on. You fucked up and you don't want yo girl to find out. Now you over there trying to figure out how you gone piece everything together. Who you think you be talking to?" I said.

"Ok Shamika, if that's the case…you knew what it was, so stop trying to blame me for everything" he said.

"And you knew the 4 years you were messing around with me. I get pregnant, you run, then blame my son…nigga please! Any who, I'm taking my baby to see his grandma so give me the address" I said.

"I ain't giving you shit. Call child support and ask them. Now you can take that baby over there if you want to. You gone get your feelings hurt by my mama. She gone turn yo goofy ass right back around" he said.

"First you say she's a sweet person now you making her seem evil. I don't believe nothing you say. I'll find out the address, I'm still taking him over there. If she rejects him…at least I tried" I said.

Although, I stated that I would still take Keith to meet his grandma, I didn't go. I was indecisive, Karter probably was right about his mother. He did everything in his power to make it like his family and mother was evil for me to keep Keith away. I decided to keep him on child support and leave everything alone.

Retrieving from thoughts

Thinking about all of that has taken place, I realized that this was nobody but God. He finally answered my prayer, not on my timing but his. I immediately replied to Ellis on Facebook.

"Hey, I think it would be great for you to be a part of Keith's life. Whenever you are ready, just let me know. We can set something up for you both to meet. Thank you for reaching out"

After messaging her I decided to take a nap. Due to me working overnights, I had to get as much rest as possible. While sleeping, I had a dream that I was walking and talking with God.

"Father, I don't want to die can you come and get me like you did the Prophet Elijah?" I asked.

Scripture provided from the bible to help readers understand what the author was asking for

As they were walking along and talking, suddenly a chariot of fire appeared, drawn by horses of fire. It drove between the two men, separating them, and Elijah was carried by a whirlwind into heaven. -2 Kings 2:11 NLT

"Yes, but only if you do right" he responded.

Then, he wrapped his arms around me as we walked down a narrow path. I woke up feeling so good. That was the first dream I had that wasn't dealing with witchcraft. The dream felt so amazing. It had been a long time since I felt that way. Checking my phone, I had numerous missed calls from Prophetess Blind. I also received another message on Facebook from Ellis. I opened the message.

"Hey Shamika, how does this Wednesday sound? I can stop by or we can meet somewhere before I go to work" she said.

"Sure. Wednesday sounds great" I replied.

I messaged her my number to call me on that day. I, then decided to call Prophetess Blind back.

"Hey! You called? I said.

"Hey, well you sound excited. What's going on with you? I didn't hear from you this morning" she said.

"Everything is fine! I have some great news! You are not going believe this. I will tell you when I see you Sunday" I said.

"Is that so? Ok, well I was just checking on you. I will see you soon" she said.

Sunday arrived, and I was so excited to get to Prophetess Blind house. I couldn't wait to tell her about the dream I had about me and God. I was anxious to share what happened regarding Keith's grandmother reaching out as well. On my way to service I was so full of joy. I knew that it was nobody but God who was moving in my life.

I just kept thinking about that dream that I had with me and him walking and talking. I felt so good and I just knew Prophetess Blind would be so excited for me. When I arrived at her house, she was in her office sitting at her desk.

"Ok, so before we get started what was it that you had to tell me" she said.

"I will start off with the dream I had. It's crazy because this was the first dream I had that didn't deal with witchcraft" I said.

"Really?" she asked.

"Yes. Ok so I was walking next to God which seemed like a spirit. I asked him can he come get me like he did the Prophet Elijah. He said he would come and get me only if I did right. We hugged and kept walking down this clear narrow path. I felt so amazing and when I woke up it felt so real" I said.

"Wow!" she said.

"Yes! I was stunned. I knew that was nobody but God" I said.

"I want to tell you a story" she said.

"Ok" I replied.

"I remember the first church I joined. There was this woman, she was very sweet. I can't think of her name but anyway she would talk to me about her dreams. I looked up to her and begin to trust her. I started telling her all my dreams. I guess she felt some sort of way that God wasn't showing her what he was showing me. When I would tell her things, she would always tell me the opposite of what my dreams meant, it would always be something bad. I, then, decided to just keep my dreams to myself. This woman was not what she seemed to be. I thank God because he kept me and showed me her true colors" she said.

"Wow! That's crazy! Why would she do that?" I asked.

"Baby girl, that's how people are. I shared this with you to tell you to be careful who you share your dreams with. A lot of people won't understand what God is doing in your life. They will mislead you by telling you otherwise. Keep your dreams to yourself" she said.

"Ok" I said.

"Well let's get started with training. We don't have much longer before service begins" she said.

During service, I noticed that Malcolm and Anna didn't show up. Sometimes they came and sometimes they didn't. It wasn't a big deal to me, yet Prophetess Blind was very frustrated.

"They don't call or nothing. At least let me know you not coming. People just do what they want to do. I'm just tired of it all" she said.

"Well maybe something came up and they couldn't make it" I responded.

"Shamika, would it have been hard for one of them to let me know that? No, it wouldn't have. It's alright, I will let God deal with them. I am tired of trying to constantly explain myself" she said.

"Yea, you right. Well let me get out of here" I said.

"Wait! Isn't there something else you have to tell me? she asked.

"Oh, yes! I almost forgot" I said.

"Ok, so Keith's grandma reached out to me over Facebook. She stated that too much time has been wasted. She desires to be a part of Keith's life. I agreed, so we set up a date for this Wednesday, so they can meet. This was something that I prayed for back when Keith was 3months old. I believe now is the time" I explained.

"Shamika, this is not the Will of God. Do you see what's going on here? We are getting closer to the move to

North Carolina and the enemy is busy. The enemy is trying to stop you from doing the Will of God" she said.

"I don't understand. It's not like I reached out to her. She reached out to me asking to be a part of her grandson. What's wrong with them building a bond? What could possibly go wrong with my son meeting his grandmother?" I said.

"Shamika, I am just trying to help. I just don't want anything to distract you from the move to North Carolina. If they build a bond now, she will want to see him a lot more than often. Listen, leave that alone. If it was meant to happen it would've happened back, then. Trust me, your boys will be fine. Keith will have a grandmother who loves and accepts him once we make it to North Carolina. What's more important, The Will of God or their relationship?" she said.

"I believe that this is the Will of God. I prayed for this to happen when Keith was still in his newborn stages. It didn't happen on my time. I'm sure this is the time God chose for it to happen. Moving to North Carolina will not stop anything. If she wants to see him, she can come visit him whenever she like" I said.

"I think it's best for God to show you himself. Starting Monday go on a 7 day fast. From 6am-6pm, drink nothing

~ 93 ~

but water. Don't eat anything and no social media. I hope you're ready because he is definitely going to show you" she said.

"Ok" I responded.

"Every time I share something exciting with her, she takes away the joy of it all. Anything I do is never the Will of God yet everything she say is. Something is not making sense. Why wouldn't God want my son to meet his grandmother? I prayed for this" I thought to myself.

I started the fast-regarding Keith and his grandma relationship on Monday. I wasn't really expecting to hear from God. Deep down, I knew this was his Will. I didn't think the enemy had nothing to do with this. If the enemy was involved, I don't think Ellis would've reached out. The week went by so fast, before I knew it, Wednesday arrived.

Ellis called me first thing Wednesday morning.

"Hey Shamika! I'm sorry but today is not going to be a good day. Can we reschedule?" she said.

Laying in my bed, tired from just getting off work, I agreed.

"Sure, no problem! Just let me know whenever you're ready" I responded.

"Ok, I will do that. Thank You. I will talk to you soon" she said.

"Things come up and there is nothing I can do about that. When the timing is right my baby and his grandma will meet and bond like never before" I thought to myself.

Waking up, it felt like I never went to sleep. Looking at my phone, I had numerous missed calls from Prophetess Blind. I called her back immediately.

"Hello, is everything alright? I asked.

"Hey, Yes! Everything is fine. I was just calling to check on you. How did everything go with Keith's grandmother?" she said.

"We didn't meet today. She asked me if we can reschedule because something came up" I said.

"See what I'm saying? Nothing came up, she just didn't want to do things on your time. She is just like her son. If I were you I would leave that alone. It's all just a distraction" she said.

"What do you mean she just didn't want to do what on my time? She is the one who set everything up, not me" I said.

"Ok, well you have 4 more days for God to show you. Have you heard from him yet regarding this situation?" she asked.

"No, not yet. That's weird because it never takes him long to answer me" I said.

"Just keep fasting he will answer before it's over" she said.

"Ok." I responded.

"Listen, I wanted to talk to you about something. The time is approaching fast for us to move to North Carolina. I know you haven't told your family. Do you plan on telling them? If so, when? Also, have you started searching for a place to stay and a job in North Carolina?" she asked.

"Yes, I know it's coming. No, I haven't told anyone just yet. I guess I will announce the move on Facebook... Thanksgiving Day. I haven't started looking for a place to stay or a job. Maybe I can see if I can get a transfer from my job to a location over there, if they have one. I'm really not sure where to start looking" I responded.

"Yes! That will be perfect, you know Diana and Terry lives in Wilson, NC. They say the cities are small and close to each other. You should ask her to help you search for a place. Be sure to only search for apartments in Greenville, NC" she said.

"Ok, I will look into everything and I will get back to you." I said.

"Ok baby girl, I will talk to you later" she said.

As soon as I got off the phone, I got right to it. I messaged Diana on Facebook.

"Hey Diana, can you send me any resources to help me find apartments in Greenville, NC. Also, do you know of any jobs that maybe hiring in that location?" I asked.

Whenever Prophetess Blind told me to do something, I would always get right to it. Although, lately I've been feeling weird about her for whatever reason, I trusted her. Diana didn't respond right away but I knew that she would. That day I decided to switch shifts with one of my co-workers. I was willing to work their morning shift if they worked my overnight shift. I was tired, I just didn't have any strength to work that night.

The next day, during my break at work I decided to take a nap. As soon as I nodded off, I instantly felt like someone was choking and smothering me at the same time.

I hopped up sweating only to realize it was just a dream. Not really thinking about it, I slowly nodded off again.

I dreamed that I was picking up Keith from his grandma house. As I was leaving, Karter's girlfriend started fighting me. As I fought back, I hit her so hard that I killed her. I ran away to the end of the next corner. As I looked back, I couldn't believe what I had just done. I hopped up by the sound of my alarm, sweating again.

"Was this dream confirmation that it's not God's Will for Keith to meet his grandma" I thought to myself.

Back at home, the only thing that was on my mind was the dream that I had. Laying in my bed, I decided to call Prophetess Blind.

"Hello" I said,

"Hey baby girl, how was work?" she asked.

"It was alright." I said.

"Oh ok, Is everything alright? Why do you sound so down?" she asked.

"You were right, it's not the Will of God for Keith to meet his grandma" I cried.

"And how do you know this? What happened?" she asked.

"I had a dream during my break. It scared the mess out of me." I said.

"Ok, what happened in this dream?" she asked.

"I was picking Keith up from his grandma house and Karter girlfriend instantly begin to fight me. I hit her so hard that I killed her then I ran away. Looking back, I felt bad because I couldn't believe what happened. Before that dream, I nodded off and instantly I felt like someone was trying to smother me to death. I couldn't breathe or move. What is going on with me?! I can't sleep and I'm constantly having all these witchcraft dreams! I'm just tired. What harm is it going to be if my baby meets his grandma! That dream was evil! I don't think that was from God! I yelled.

"Shamika, calm down. Didn't I explain to you last week that God was going to show you that this was not his Will? And what to do mean the dream was evil and it wasn't from God? He was showing you all the things that will take place if Keith meets his grandmother. I also explained to you that those are witchcraft dreams that you are having. You need to pray against it and it will go away" she said.

"But I have been praying! I keep having them! I never had these many dreams back to back like this in my life. I'm steady going to sleep waking up like I never went to sleep. Am I doing something wrong because I have no peace!" I yelled.

"No, you are not doing anything wrong. It takes time" she said.

"Ok, I'm about to go to sleep. None of this is making sense to me" I said.

"Ok, get you some rest and make sure you tell Keith's grandmother that it's not the Will of God for them to meet. I don't want you to linger her on for something that's not going to happen" she said.

After getting off the phone with Prophetess Blind, I laid in my bed crying.

"WHY?! WHY?! WHY?! MY GOD! WHY?! What could possibly go wrong if my baby met his grandma? Would this really stop me from moving to North Carolina? Jesus, what is going on me with me and the people around me? Are they really who they say they are? Why every time I share something with my pastor she makes everything seem so wrong? Father God, what is your Will for me? Please show me! I am tired of these witchcraft dreams. I don't have any peace! I am still broken, and

things only seem to be getting worse. Father your word says; *The Lord is close to the brokenhearted; he rescues those whose spirits are crushed. Psalms 34:18 NLT*
Please help me, deliver me and set me free from whatever is going on, In Jesus name, Amen." I prayed.

> *Would I ever bring this nation to the point of birth and then not deliver it?" asks the Lord. "No! I would never keep this nation from being born," says your God.*
> *-Isaiah 66:9 NLT*

Immediately after praying, I fell into a deep sleep. I had two dreams that left me confused. The first dream I had, Diana was furious and yelling at me about something. I couldn't hear the exact words that she was saying. Behind her stood Prophetess Blind. They both were wearing all black. While Diana was yelling at me, Prophetess Blind fell in a slow motion behind her.

I hopped up from the dream sweating and looking around. Laying down, I instantly went into the second dream. I was laying in my bed and there were snakes all around me. They were moving really slow while staring at me. I got up and ran out of my room and shut the door so that they wouldn't get out. I started looking for my babies, but they were nowhere in sight.

Headed towards the front door, snakes where coming from every direction but they didn't touch me. I opened the front door to leave my house. Immediately something that I couldn't see picked me up and threw me down the hallway. It threw me so hard that I knew if I landed I wasn't going to make it. I screamed, "JESUS! HELP ME!" then I woke up.

Laying in my bed, I was afraid to move. I didn't know what was going on in those dreams. The dream that stood out to me the most is when Diana was yelling at me and Prophetess Blind fell behind her.

"I wonder why Diana was so angry with me. I'm confused, she is such a sweet person. I just don't understand, maybe it's just the enemy" I thought to myself.

I couldn't call anyone to discuss those dreams, not even Prophetess Blind. She explained to me to keep my dreams to myself, so I did just that.

Finally, I decided to get up and go pick my babies up from school. Looking at my phone, I had a missed call from Ellis and numerous missed calls from Prophetess Blind. There wasn't a day that went by that I didn't have a missed call from Prophetess Blind. I really didn't want to return Ellis phone call. I just wasn't sure how I was going to tell her that her and Keith couldn't meet. Sitting in my living room before I left out, I called Prophetess Blind back.

"Hey Baby girl, is everything alright?" she said.

"Hey, yes everything is fine" I said.

"Oh ok, I was calling to talk to you about something, is now alright for you?" she asked.

"Yes" I responded.

"Are you sure you're alright? You just don't sound like yourself" she said.

"Yes, I'm alright" I said.

"Ok, I was thinking, if you are going to be my armorbearer you need to talk to me every day about everything. I say this because it's your responsibility to get to know me. I just want you to know what to do and how to do it. If we were to ever go out to church meetings and events, you should know exactly what to do. I know that we are doing training every week; however, it's time for physical training. Elder Blind will be able to teach you that part. He himself was an armorbearer first before he became a Pastor. So, tell me what's your thoughts?" she said.

"Ok that's fine with me whenever you ready just let me know. As far as the talking to you daily we already talk daily, so what do you mean by that?" I said.

"I know but I find myself calling you a lot more and sometimes you don't answer. You be over there hiding honey" she laughed.

"Ok. So, you want me to make it my business to call and check on you?" I asked.

"Yes. We don't have to be on the phone for long. You're just calling to see how my day went and so on. If something should come up with me or you, then we can discuss it" she explained.

"Ok" I said.

"One more thing before you go, how is the apartment searching going? Did you reach out to Diana so that she can help you?" she asked.

"Yes. I messaged her on Facebook right after you told me to. She hasn't responded yet. I figured she will when she has time" I said.

"You see that's exactly what I'm talking about. She doesn't take this ministry seriously. When it come to her job, school and family, she gets it done. However, anything regarding God and this ministry, she does things on her time. Folk do what they want to do. When God gives me the word to rebuke and release them, they be wondering why. Well, baby girl continue searching for whatever you can find, until she responds. I will ask her about it for you" she said.

"Ok" I responded.

Chapter Five

I was starting to realize that every time I told Prophetess Blind something that was outside of her expectations, she would throw a tantrum and get angry. Everything that everyone did always was a problem. She talked bad about them all. Although I was beginning to realize this I didn't say anything. I started to wonder was she talking about me like she did others.

Later that day, I decided to switch shifts and work the next morning. I was getting tired of working overnights. I went from loving it to being drained by it. I was there alone and on top of that I kept getting attacked in my dreams while on break. I just didn't want to deal with that. I was dealing with enough at home already. That night before bed, I texted Ellis.

"Hey, whenever the time is right for you, please give me a call. It's regarding Keith"

Now I wasn't expecting to talk to her that night, but she called me shortly after.

"Hey Shamika, I just got off work. How is my grandbaby? Is everything alright?" she said.

Ellis was always so full of Joy. She was an amazing woman. I really didn't understand why God wouldn't want her to be a part of Keith. I didn't want God to be angry with me, so I had to tell her.

"Hey, Keith is alright, and everything is fine. I wanted to talk to you about you and Keith relationship. Now I prayed for this back when Keith was 3 months. I fasted for this and spoke to my pastor about it. She stated that it's not God's Will for you to be a part of his life. I know that she would not tell me anything wrong. Lately it's just been a lot of drama with Karter and this whole situation. I just think it best that I stand clear from it all. I'm sorry but you can't meet Keith. It's just not right, I'm sorry" I explained.

"But I love him. What do you mean? Why wouldn't God want this for my grandbaby? He needs to know me, I'm his grandmother. He needs to know his family. We love him. Listen, I know that my son has rejected him. I don't understand why he would this to him. We don't do that in this family but all I can do is what I can as his grandmother" She said.

"I understand but it's not the Will of God" I said.

There was a moment of silence before Ellis responded.

"Ok, I don't understand any of this, but I know you know what's best for your son. I will be praying for you and my grandbaby. I love you both and if you ever change your mind, please just call me" she said.

"Ok." I responded.

When I got off the phone, I couldn't help but to cry. Although I was explaining to Ellis that it wasn't the Will of God, I felt different. It all just felt so wrong.

"Father God, is this really your Will? If so, why do I feel this way? I feel like it was the wrong thing to do. Father, can you please just hold me?" I prayed.

That night I slept like a baby. If I did have a dream I couldn't remember it, I slept so peaceful. Although I knew God, I didn't know him enough to hear him speak. I was indecisive regarding certain information or dreams. I didn't know if it was from God or the enemy. I was at a point in my life where I wanted to know him.
I wanted to get in his face and have long conversations with only him. I really didn't have anyone else to talk to other than Prophetess Blind. She told me to keep my dreams to myself. I felt that maybe she was tired of me sharing certain things with her. I was still suffering with the unforgiveness that I refused to let go towards my mother. The hurt lingered deeply regarding Karter rejecting my son. It all

still bothered me. I just wanted to forgive, let go and be free from it all.

I was doing everything Prophetess Blind said is pleasing in the sight of the Lord. However, I was still broken deep within. I thought that it would all go away yet it all just seem to get worse. I got up at 4am by the sound of my alarm for prayer. Getting on the prayer line, I noticed that it was just me and Prophetess Blind again.

Malcolm, Anna, Diana and Terry would get on sometimes. Other times they would get on late and most times not at all. Tia got on every now and then. After prayer, I headed straight to work. I really liked working the morning shift 6am-2pm. While at work I spoke to my manager regarding a shift change.

"Hey Marie, I was wondering if I can switch from my overnight shift to this morning shift? I said.

"Hey Shamika, I am glad you mentioned this. I am working on a change within everyone's schedule. I wasn't sure if you wanted a morning shift or if you preferred overnights. So, are you alright with a 6am-2pm shift for now on?" she asked.

"Yes! That would be perfect for me" I responded.

"Ok, I won't be posting the new schedule until next Friday" she said.

"Ok, Thank You. One more thing, I will be moving to Greenville, North Carolina around the Spring of 2017. Is there any way that I can get transferred to a location over there?" I asked.

"Oh my God! Congratulation! I do know that we have a location in North Carolina. I'm not sure if it's Greenville. I will look into that for you and let you know" she said.

"Ok. Thank you so much" I said.

I was so excited that my manager was switching my shift. Only God knew how bad I really wanted to get away from my overnight shift. For the rest of the day, I felt so good. Everything went well for the first time in a long time. I hadn't spoken to Prophetess Blind, but I didn't mind.

The following Tuesday, which was my off day, I decided to take a walk to the lake. During my teenager years, I use to go to the lake a lot. I would stare at the water, cry, and release everything I was dealing with. It had been a long time since I've been there and done that. On my way to the lake Prophetess Blind called me.

"Hey baby girl, what are you doing?"

"Hey, not much, just headed to the lake. What are you doing? I said.

"Well me and Elder Blind are headed to Kmart to pay on our Christmas layaway. We are really trying to hold on to it as much as possible, so we pay something little by little every chance we get" she explained.

"Aw ok. How much more do you have to pay before you can take it out?" I asked.

"Let me get the receipt and see. Hold on one second……Ok, I have a total of $284.00. That's just to keep it where they don't cancel it out. We are going up there now to put a little down on it but it's nowhere near that amount. Hopefully they will work something out with us" she said.

"Aw ok, well if you can't pay that amount for whatever reason, you know you can always just cancel the layaway and get all your money back" I said.

"Yes, I'm aware of that. The things that I have are my kids Christmas toys and a majority of house needs" she said.

"Do you really need it or is it something that you really want? The kids will be fine, they will understand. I mean if you don't have it, you just don't have it. At least you can get your money back and use that to go out or something" I said.

"Shamika, I have a big family $200 is not enough to do anything. That explains why a lot of times me and my husband just go out without the kids. It's just not enough for everyone. I don't know if I told you, but we are going through bankruptcy. We are almost done paying due to it coming directly out of my husband's check. With him working at Walmart we aren't really left with much. We barely have money to pay our bills. I have been trying to see what Tia is going to do regarding her tithing because she still hasn't paid them. She keeps saying she must ask her husband. Anytime she needs anything she don't have to ask him, she just buy it. It's frustrating at times because when people continuously refuse to obey God, it makes me look bad. I keep trying to talk to Tia and explain this to her. She just keeps telling me the same thing. However, when God releases her, there is nothing I can do about that" she explained.

"Wow, I wonder what's really the problem behind her refusing to pay her tithes" I said.

"There is no problem, folk just want to do what they want to do. When I say something about money people get quiet and start acting crazy. When they need prayer, they expect me jump for them. What people fail to realize is that they are not giving me anything they are giving unto the Lord. When they don't give there is nothing I can do about that, God will deal with them. Now does that mean I have to stop doing what God called me to do? Absolutely not. I have to keep moving forward with or without" she said.

"Yes. At times that's all you can do is continue to move forward. I understand where you're coming from. I'm sorry that you're going through this" I said.

"It's alright baby girl, I am glad that I don't have these problems with you. You have always paid your tithes and offerings on time and you make sure you sow a seed. I just wish everyone could be faithful in giving like you are. Then I will not have these problems" she laughed.

"I will see what I can do once I get paid. If I have it to give, I will pay your layaway off for you" I said.

"Really! Are you sure?" she asked.

"Yes" I said.

"Thank You so much. God is going to bless you for this" she said.

"No problem" I responded.

"Here is why I really called you. I wanted to talk to you about being my armorbearer. Now as you know, we are already in the month of November and the woman's conference is approaching. I just wanted to inform you that for every event I go to, I do get paid for it. Now whatever I get paid, you will get a portion of that pay as well" she said.

"Really? I didn't know that" I said.

"Yes, baby girl. Anything that I receive you get half. You are working to protect me. So, like at the woman's conference, I believe......

Prophetess Blind was interrupted.

"WHOA! WHOA! WHOA!" shouted Elder Blind.

"What's wrong baby!? What was that all about?" she asked.

"Wait a minute, hold on for a second Shamika" she said.

When Prophetess Blind placed me on hold, I thought over our whole conversation. It never fails every time my payday was approaching, she called with a story regarding money. She had a way of asking without asking, if you know what I mean. I always felt so guilty as if I had to do something about her problems. I believed she knew that and took advantage of it.
After being on hold for a long time, Prophetess Blind got back on the phone. She started talking about something that

had nothing to do with an armorbearer and the woman's conference.

"What are you doing? Oh! That's right you're at the lake" she said.

Although I was confused as to why we didn't finish having our conversation, I just went along with her.

"Yes. I'm still here at the lake. I think I might be getting ready to head back home though" I said.

"Oh ok. Have you been on face book lately?" she asked.

"No. why do you ask that?" I said.

"I was asking because I saw Malcolm and Anna on there half naked in the bed snapping pictures. I was just wondering what's your thoughts as my armorbearer?" she said.

"Oh wow! Well it's not much that you can do. Just pray for them and hopefully they will slow down with doing the things that you don't like" I responded.

"Shamika, do you realize when you all do things it makes me look bad? It's like I'm not teaching anything. It's like I allow anything in this ministry, but I don't" she said.

"I understand but why do you beat yourself up when someone refuse to listen. If you're doing what God called you to do while continuing to pray, that's all that matters" I said.

"Yes, I know that's the same thing my husband said. Sometimes I just feel like I'm doing something wrong because everyone is still doing the same thing. I refuse to be like Moses. He allowed the people of Israel to make him angry with God" she said.

"Just keep doing what you've been doing and let God deal with his people" I said.

"Yes, you're right. Well baby girl, go on with your day. I will talk to you tomorrow" she said.

"Alright" I responded.

After my conversation with Prophetess Blind, I kept trying to think about what Elder Blind said to make her change the subject. I wonder was it about giving me a portion as her armorbearer. Although, she would always say "when people give, they give to God and not to her" her actions never added up with what she said.
She would always get so angry and frustrated when it came down to tithings, offerings and even sowing seeds. I was starting to believe that she talks badly about me as well. She always had something to say about everyone but me.

Unless, she talked about me to everyone else or maybe just
Tia and Diana. I'm not sure but I was beginning to feel
weird and I didn't know why.

As time went on, my work scheduled changed to mornings.
I found out that there was no way that I could be transferred
to Greenville, NC. The nearest location was Charlotte, NC.
According to Prophetess Blind that location was too far and
not the Will of God. This led me to be even more busy. I
was getting up for prayer at 4am, while having to be at
work by 6am.

I spent the remaining of my days searching for apartments
and jobs in Greenville, NC. I was exhausted. I never had a
day off even on my normal off days. I had to make sure I
called and checked on Prophetess Blind daily. This
weighed me down even more because all she did was
complain. I was on top of everything as if I had it all under
control, but I really didn't.

While still suffering bad on the inside, I was stressed out.
The witchcraft dreams only got worse, along with sleepless
nights. Diana had finally responded to my message
regarding her helping me search for a place and a job. It
still felt like I was doing everything on my own. The
woman's conference was a week away. Malcom and
Anna's wedding were two weeks away.

My payday was around the corner, however I was never
excited about it. I was giving a majority of my check to
tithes, offerings and sowing seeds. There were times where
I had to keep pushing my bills back to make sure I paid my

tithes. At times, I really didn't have enough to give an offering or sow a seed. Prophetess Blind demanded that no matter what I had to do it. It had gotten to the point where I would get off work and come straight home. My house was dry and almost empty because I kept giving away everything to Prophetess Blind. I kept seeing her kids wear and play with everything I brought to her house for the clothes drive.

Nothing was beginning to make sense. I was seeing what was going on, yet I was unable to say anything about it. I've never been quiet to strange or suspicious things. I have always been outspoken. This situation was different. All I was able to do was remain quiet, listen very well and observe every detail.

The woman's conference was approaching fast and so was my payday. One morning before work, I was in bed thinking about buying me something nice to wear. It had been awhile since I've done anything for me and my boys. I thought it would be alright to do so, while searching for my outfit and shoes online, I received a text message from Prophetess Blind.

It was early in the morning, so I thought it might have been something wrong. When I opened the text message it was a picture of a dress. The dress was a bright carol color, long and beautiful. Although I viewed the text, I didn't respond instead I started getting ready for work.

"Why would she send me a picture of a dress at 5am in the morning?" I thought to myself.

After a long day of work, I checked my phone to a missed call from Prophetess Blind. I decided to call her back once I made it home. Driving home, I realized that Thanksgiving was near. It was almost time for me to make the announcement. Once I made it home, I laid down to rest before it was time to go back out to get my babies from school. While nodding off to sleep, Prophetess Blind called me, I answered.

"Hey Shamika, what are you doing?" she said.

"Hey, nothing much just got in from work. What's going on with you?" I responded.

"Nothing. I was just calling to see if you received my text message. I also wanted to talk to you about something" she said.

"Yes, I received it. I was getting ready for work, so I couldn't respond. I was looking forward to calling you back after work, but I decided to rest instead. It's a good thing you called me. Is everything alright?" I said.

"It's alright baby girl, I know you have a lot going on. Everything is fine I just wanted to tell you to make sure that when you are sending your tithes, offerings and sowing of seeds, make sure you notate what it's for. I just want to be sure of everything and not get anything mixed up. Also, I sent you the dress because I wanted to know your thoughts. I actually sent you two, I am trying to find me something nice to wear to the woman's conference" she said.

"Ok. I will make sure I note it. I always do though but I will be very clear this time around. I think the dress is beautiful. I like the carol one but that's the only one I received" I said.

"Really? I sent you a black one too. They're both the same, just an assorted color. So, you think I should get the carol one?" she asked.

"Yes. That one will bring out your skin tone. What kind of shoes were you thinking about wearing?" I asked.

"Yes. I like that one too. I was thinking the same thing. I was just looking at some black flats because you know my legs gets weak after a while. I wouldn't be able to do anything with a heel" she said.

"Aw ok. You already prepared!" I laughed.

"Yes, I know. Hopefully if everyone pays their tithes on time and my husband have a little money leftover, I can order it. However, the thing is it takes 7 days to get here and the woman's conference is next Saturday. I know Diana and Terry normally pay their tithes on a Monday.

Tia, I am not sure about. My husband gets paid the day before the event, so that won't help at all" she explained.

"Wow ok! It's crazy because I was just looking for me something to wear. However, I will buy the dress and shoes for you. I will send you the money when I get paid to order the dress. I will go one day next week during my break to get your shoes. I don't have anything to wear but I will be fine" I said.

"OMG! Are you sure?" she asked.

"Yes. I'm sure. Don't worry about it but let me take a nap before I pick up my boys. I will talk to you later" I said.

"Ok. I appreciate you. Remember don't forget to notate what you are giving when you send your tithes and offerings" she said.

"Ok" I responded.

Laying in my bed, I replayed back our entire conversation.

"Every time I get paid it never fails. She always calls me with a story about something. It always requires me to give more money. It's like she waits for me to offer so she doesn't have to ask. Wait a minute, did she say that she is basically waiting on everyone to pay their tithes so that she can handle a personal need? I thought tithes and offerings go specially towards the church needs only. Ok, let me stop thinking like this, maybe this is the enemy playing with my mind" I thought to myself.

Friday came, and it was payday. I made sure I paid my tithes, offerings, and sowing of seeds. I sent Prophetess Blind the money for the dress, which was $60. That covered the dress and shipping fees as well. During the following week, I stopped at payless and brought her some black flats. I then, dropped them off to her and she was all set for the woman's conference that Saturday. I was so jaded. I couldn't wait to this woman's conference; wedding and this whole move thing was over with.

The day before the woman's conference, I had no one to watch my boys for me. I called and asked my mom can my sister come over, however she took her to my aunt house instead. I texted Prophetess Blind and explained to her what was going on. I explained to her that I wasn't going to be able to attend the woman's conference. Later that night as I was preparing for bed, when Prophetess Blind called me.

"Hey, did you find someone to watch the boys?" she asked.

"No. My mom didn't bring my sister over. She took her to my aunt house instead" I said.

"My husband has to work tomorrow, and he can't miss any days. It's crazy that I'm not going to have anyone from this ministry to support me" she said disheartened.

There was silence on the phone because I had nothing to say. To be honest, I really didn't have enough gas and I didn't want to go. I didn't understand why I didn't want to go, it was something in me that just didn't feel right.

"She is your armorbearer! She needs to figure something out! I have to work, I can't take you. I can pick you up, but I can't take you. As your armorbearer, it's her responsibility to make a way for you and be there with you!" yelled Elder Blind.

"How is your husband not able to take you or support you at a special event like this? If it's anybody responsibility, it should be his. He should be making a way. What does he mean it's my responsibility as your armorbearer? The last time I checked I was still in training. I haven't even learned the physical training as an armorbearer yet. I don't have a babysitter! What am I supposed to do?" I thought to myself.

"Maybe you can bring the boys over here. My daughter will watch them for you" she said.

Now Prophetess Blind wasn't a nasty person. She depended on her kids to do the cleaning around her house. They cleaned but not the right way. I went there for armorbearer training and service on Sundays. I wouldn't dare go there on any other day. Neither would I let my boys go there while I'm not with them. I trusted her but not with my babies. When she said they can come over I just remained quiet on the phone.

"I will figure something out. I will call you back" I said.

"Ok" she responded.

"She obviously just doesn't care that I don't have a babysitter. Now I have to figure out something out of nothing" I thought to myself.

It was 10 o'clock at night. I woke my babies up and head to my aunt house to pick up my sister. I didn't make it back in the house until 11:45pm that night. I took a hot shower, set my alarm to 6am and went to sleep. The next morning, I woke up by the sound of my alarm, threw something on and headed straight to Prophetess Blind house. I arrived at her house at 7am we didn't have to be to the woman's conference until 9am. The woman's conference was all the way on 125th and Kedzie, so I was hoping she would be ready to go. When Prophetess Blind opened the front door to let me in, I was excited to see how beautiful she would look in the dress I brought her. When I walked inside the house she was wearing a black maxi dress with a white shirt underneath. I was confused,

"Ok maybe she'll put her clothes on when she's done with her makeup" I thought to myself.

"See I don't like this. I just feel so uncomfortable and I don't have anything to wear" she said.

"What do she mean she don't have anything to wear?" I thought to myself.

I sat there in silence as she got ready. I was wondering where was the dress that I gave her the money for. While waiting on her to get ready I noticed a tote in front of me with a lot of new packs of hair in it. After glancing at the hair, I looked up and Prophetess Blind was staring at me. She than begin to talk,

"I am going to need you to have patience. One thing about me is I am never on time. I had a dream you came early though" she laughed.

Looking at the clock it was already 8:15am, she decided to change into this blue flower dress and we headed out at 8:30am. During the conference, when it was time for Prophetess Blind to speak she seemed very nervous. She kept moving around and sweating very bad.

"Is this her first time speaking in front of others?" I thought to myself.

She would always say that she council a lot of people and have church meetings to go to. I didn't know what that meant because she wasn't apart of anyone's church. However, I wasn't expecting her to react this way at the woman's conference. As her armorbearer I just sat there and listened as she spoke. I didn't know what to do and so I didn't do anything. I kept seeing a young lady bring her water and napkins every so often.

"Is that what I'm supposed to be doing as an armorbearer?" I thought to myself.

Still unsure I just sat there quietly listening and observing my surroundings. When the conference was over Prophetess Blind received an envelope. Soon after Elder Blind was there to pick her up. I wasn't quite sure how to get back. I assumed I could just follow them at least until I was safe back into the city. I helped Prophetess Blind into the passenger side of Elder Blind car and I immediately got into my car. As they pulled off following their lead, I noticed that they were driving very fast and constantly switching lanes.

"What is going on? Do they not want me to follow them back into the city? I don't even know where I'm at or how to get back home?" I thought to myself.

Before I knew it, they vanished. I was left finding my own way back home. It took me 2 ½ hours to get back home safely. By the time I made it home my gas hand was on E. Sitting in my car before I went inside, I cried in silence.

"Now where am I going to get gas money from. How am I constantly going to work but always broke? I am so tired, GOD IM TIRED! IM TIRED OF FEELING THIS WAY! I don't have any money, no gas, I barely have any food and my house doesn't even feel like a home. I can't believe they left me and didn't even call to see if I made it home. I wonder what was in that envelope…naw you know what let me stop… the least she could've did was see if I needed some gas. You know what just stop Shamika! Just Stop! God how am I supposed to get to work for the next two weeks? How?!" I cried.

I sat in my car for about 30 minutes talking to myself and crying out to God. I couldn't let my babies and my sister see me like this. Walking in the house seeing my boys made me feel so good. Their faces always brightened up what seem like darkness in my life. David was my Joy and Keith was my Strength. My boys kept me going even at times when I really wanted to give up.

After showering, I felt so debilitated. Laying down, it felt as if someone pulled my soul out of me because for a minute I couldn't move. With the little strength in me, I slid down from my bed onto my knees. I placed my face down and stretched my arms on the floor.

"Father God, I just want to say thank you. Thank you for keeping me. During this place in my life I feel like I need a breakthrough. I feel like I'm moving but I'm not accomplishing anything. It's like I'm not going anywhere. I feel like I'm in a dark place but the only light I have at this moment is you. The only one I have and always had by my side is you. I need you more than anything right now. My body is weak, and I can barely even talk right now. I can't take it anymore. I know I've said this before but father I really can't take it anymore. I can't handle it anymore. I surrender all to you right now in Jesus name. Father, all I ask is for more of your Grace to put the effort into breaking free and serving your purpose. Father, I just want more of you and I desire to do your Will, not my own or anyone else. Father, I come before you as boldly and humble as I know how. I repent of every thought, action and words, that was presented and spoken from me on this day. Father God, take me by my hand and lead me down the path that you have created for me, the path of everlasting life. The path of freedom, peace and love. Father God, place your hand over my mind and renew it. Allow me to have your discernment and perception as you guide me from this day forward. Father, before I go all I ask is that you grant me more of your Grace to remain faithful and obedient unto you. All I want is more of you, all I desire is to be a faithful woman after your heart. Father God, I promise that if you just show me…Please, just show me your Will for me, no matter what I will grab hold to it and never let it go. Thank You Father God, In Jesus mighty name, I pray. Amen"

Teach me your decrees, Oh Lord; I will keep them to the end. Give me understanding and I will obey your instructions; I will put them into practice with all my heart.
-Psalms 119:33-34 NLT

That night I slept like a baby, it felt as if someone with huge warm soft arms held me all night long. I was awakened the next morning by a call from Prophetess Blind.

"Hey baby girl, are you sleep? Did I wake you?" she asked.

"Hey, Yes. I'm sleeping" I said.

"Oh! Ok, well give me a call when you wake up" she said.

"Ok" I responded.

Normally when Prophetess Blind call while I'm sleeping, I get up for her however, this time was different. I just didn't feel like being bothered. I was starting to realize that whenever she called it was always to talk about someone apart of the ministry, tell me what I shouldn't be doing and complaining about something else that broke down in her house or car.

I was dealing with enough and it was driving me insane. We barely talked about God unless she was explaining to me what is and what's not his Will. At this point in my life, all I wanted to do was get in the face of God. I desired to hear about what he had to say about everything.

It felt so good to be able to lay in my bed and simply rest with no distractions. I decided to get up around 5pm to get my day started. I didn't call Prophetess Blind back immediately after I got up. I waited until later that night to give her a call back.

"Hey, what's going on?" I said.

"Wow! You must've really been tired. Are you just now waking up?" she said.

"No. I got up around 5pm and started doing some cleaning. Now I'm back in bed resting" I said.

"Aw ok. Well I called you to ask you as my armorbearer, what are somethings you caught on yesterday during the woman's conference? Also, how do you think I did delivering God's message?" she asked.

Now as I listened to Prophetess Blind ask me these two questions. I had to think carefully about how I would answer them both. In any conversation that I had with her and others, being honest and straight-forward was all I had to offer. It was difficult when dealing with her. If I said something that she wasn't expecting to hear, she would throw a tantrum and become frustrated.

"I think everything went well. Everyone was nice and respectful. I noticed that you were sweating and moving around a lot. I could barely hear you and you were right next me. Even though you were a bit nervous, you did a wonderful job delivering God's message" I responded.

"Oh no! I wasn't nervous baby girl. It's just that my legs get weak after standing for a long time. That also explains why I was sweating. So, you think everyone was nice, really?" she said.

"Yes, everyone was nice and welcoming from what I saw. What do you think?" I said.

"I believe that it was so easy for different woman to preach of how God is going to bless everyone. However, they all seem to leave out what we all need to do to prepare for his blessings. I am just glad God placed it on my heart to be the only one who brought forth a message regarding what needs to be done first before he overflows us with his many blessings" she said.

"Wow! I didn't pay attention to that" I said.

"Yes. And another thing did you see that after a while the woman who kept yelling out hallelujah, eventually stopped. She couldn't handle what I was preaching, see they are not use to the truth. That's why I always tell you all that after me God is not sending anyone else to save his people. It all stops after me, so baby girl continue being obedient unto the Lord" she said.

"Ok" I responded.

I never knew what Prophetess Blind was talking about when she said after her God is not sending anyone else. I believed that God could move in, work through and raise up anyone he desire to use… from a newborn baby up to a senior citizen. I just never understood what she was trying to get across by saying that.

Every time she said that to me and others apart of the ministry, I would always feel so afraid. I felt like no matter what, I had to stay close to her and be everywhere she was. She made me feel like the only way I can get close to God was through her.

"That's what I was originally calling you for. Ok, so you know Malcolm and Anna are getting married this upcoming Saturday. He came earlier today, and we went to a place near 65th and Archer, I believe; to purchase me a robe" she said.

"A robe? What kind of robe?" I asked confused.

"A choir robe, you know the robes that pastors and bishops wear in churches or during weddings" she explained.

"Aww ok. That was nice of him to do for you. Now you don't have to worry about what to wear for his wedding" I said.

"Yeah, I guess" she said nonchalantly.

"What's wrong? Why you say it like that?" I asked.

"I don't know. I just really wanted the white robe, but he got me the black one with gold linens" she said.

"Is it nice? How much was it? Did you tell him which one you wanted?" I asked.

"Well the white one was $400.00 and the black one was $200.00 roughly around $250.00 after taxes. Yes, I told him but honey you know how people are with their money. I was just grateful for this one and plus I never owned a robe before, this is my first one. I just wish I would've had enough money because I would've brought that white one" she said.

"$400.00! that's a lot for just one robe! And I know the black one was only $200.00 but that's still too much for just one robe. I thought they were like $50.00 and up. Well

I mean it's only for one day, that's probably why he decided to get you that one. That maybe the color they're wearing in their wedding" I said.

"That's not a lot and besides the way it was made was well worth the amount they were asking for. They are wearing like an off white and gold color, which is why I don't understand why he just didn't get me the white robe but it's alright" she said.

"Yes, you will be fine but let me go ahead and go to sleep. I need all the rest I can get" I said.

"Ok baby girl" she responded.

After getting off the phone with Prophetess Blind, I replayed our whole conversation over again. I'm not sure why but when it came to her, my memory was precise. I didn't forget a word spoken or an action made.

"I can't believe she complained about which robe Malcom brought her. It's bad enough her and Elder Blind technically pressured him into getting married with not much time to do anything. I don't care what anybody say, I still believe that there should have been some sort of engagement before the marriage. This way Malcom and Anna would have been able to prepare the wedding without rushing it. They would've been able to prepare for one another. I've never been married but I know for a fact it doesn't take a man 8 years to marry a woman. I knew she was going to disagree with my opinion, in which she asked for, regarding the women's conference. She so quick to say no one wants the truth but she can't seem to handle it herself. Jesus, what is going on?!" I thought to myself.

The following week for me was so stressful. I was looking for an apartment in North Carolina but couldn't seem to find anything at a reasonable price. I was lucky to finally find a two-bedroom, two-bathroom apartment for $698 a month, located in the downtown area. This location was perfect because schools, nearby stores and restaurants were walking distance, however I still needed a car.
The car that I had was problematic and I had no money to fix it. Every time I looked up Prophetess Blind seem to have plans with my whole paycheck before I even got paid. I decided that once I move to North Carolina I was going to give my car back to the dealership, it would be pointless to bring it with me. Even though I found a beautiful apartment in North Carolina, the rent was a bit expensive due to it being located downtown.
I decided that since I didn't have anything saved up, I would just use my tax refund to move there and pay off my rent 6 months in advance. I figured that by than I would at least have a job while living there. I was thinking long and hard about everything. I just didn't want to find myself stranded. This whole move thing was starting not to make sense to me.

Before I knew it, Malcolm and Anna's wedding were only one day away. Although I didn't understand how fast everything went, I was excited for them both. Marriage was a beautiful gift created by God. One day after work, Prophetess Blind called me.

"Hey Shamika, how was your day?" she said.

"Hey Pastor, my day went well and yours?" I responded.

"It was alright. Is this an appropriate time for you because I needed to talk to you?" she said.

"Yes, I just made it home from work, what's going on?" I said.

"Ok before I say what I'm about to say…. quick question; Are you still going to be able to give me the money for my Christmas layaway? I am just trying to make sure because I have to go and get it by next Tuesday" she said.

"To be honest with you, I don't even have enough money to get my kids nothing for Christmas. After I pay my tithes and offerings, I have to put what little I am going to have towards my light bill" I explained.

"Oh ok. Did you forget about what you said? How much was your check?" she asked.

"No. it's not that I forgot what I said, I just don't have enough money and I'm behind on my light bill. My check wasn't the amount that it normally would've been" I said.

"Aww ok. Are you familiar with Ceda?" she asked.

"Yes, I am very familiar with Ceda. I went to them in the beginning of this month for my lights. It takes about 3-6wks to receive any kind of payment from them. I am still responsible for paying my light bill into that kicks in" I explained.

"Aww ok, well I guess I am going to have to go and get my money back. Is this your boys first time without having a Christmas?" she said.

"No. when I was pregnant with Keith I wasn't working and so David had to go without a Christmas from me, but my family made sure he was straight. Even though I'm not going to be able to get them anything, my family always come through for my boys" I responded.

"Aww ok, well there you go. You will be alright, see I don't have that. If I can't do for my kids, they just have to go without. You know something Christmas is not even about what we believe it is. I am going to have to seek God to see if he wants me to do a bible study session on these pagan holidays" she said.

"Ok" I responded.

As I listened to Prophetess Blind talk, it's like she played the victim at first. She then turned around and made herself feel justified about the whole situation. I believe she wanted me to say forget my light bill, still pay her layaway and pay my tithes and offerings as well.

I am not sure what was going on, but I was starting to see and hear things clearer than ever. I don't know if it was God or the devil but everything I was sensing just didn't feel right.

"Oh, that's what I originally called you for. Have you spoke to your mother lately?" she asked.

"No, it's really nothing to talk to her about. I just don't have time. I rather keep things the way they are" I said.

"Shamika, this have to stop. You still have not let go of the hurt that your mother caused you. This explains why you haven't let a lot of other things go as well. There are a lot of things that are still bothering you from your past and its holding you back as well. Listen, I know that your mother hurt you and I am not saying it was right of her to do but you have to give it to God" she explained.

"I did give it to God. Which is why I am no longer dealing with it" I said.

"Ok, so if that's the cast why every time I ask about her, you get angry and refuse to talk about it?" she said.

"I don't get angry, I just don't feel the need to discuss anything regarding her" I responded.

"Shamika, Listen. I remember some years back I walked in on my mother having a phone conversation with my aunt. She told my aunt she wishes she could've just had my sisters and not me. That hurt me so bad for a long time, but I gave it all to God. To this day I love my mother regardless of what she has done to me and I will never let anyone break or come between that. I realize that she is the one with the problem, that have nothing to do with me" she explained.

"I love my mother. I just don't understand why she treat me the way she does. I sometimes feel like I'm not her daughter. She makes me feel like a stranger, like I was adopted or something. Therefore, I choose to stay away. Just because I stay away doesn't mean that I don't love her though. I love her with everything in me and I want things to be right between us. I just need time to heal and grow a clear understanding of all this" I explained.

"I understand. Have you ever been to counseling regarding this situation?" she asked.

"No" I said.

"Would you like for me to counsel you? I ask because I believe that it will help if you talked about it a little at a time" she said.

"Yes. That would be alright" I said.

"Ok, so I will counsel you every Thursday night at 7pm right before prayer at 8pm. In the meantime, I want you to write a letter to your mother about what she did and how it made you feel. Do not read the letter to her, bring it to me when you are finished" she said.

"Ok" I responded.

"Also, don't forget that tomorrow is Malcolm and Anna's wedding. It starts at 4pm so you should be headed straight this way once you get off work.

"Ok, see you tomorrow" I said.

Chapter Six

That night before bed, it was heavy on my mind why
Prophetess Blind didn't have on the dress that I brought
her. I laid in my bed and once again thoughts filled my
mind. This time I thought back to when I first met her. I
remembered every word she spoke since then. I wanted to
ask her about it, but I didn't know how. I never said or
questioned her about anything.

　　Although many people try to play me, I wasn't
imbecile to anything. I only spoke on certain issues when I
had enough evidence. In this case I felt that I had more than
enough. I was curious to know what happened. I stopped
contemplating and I decided to ask her. I messaged her on
Facebook messenger;

"Hey Pastor, You busy?" I said.

"Hey, no I'm not busy. Is everything alright?" she said.

"Yes. Everything is fine. I have a question for you" I said.

"Ok" she responded.

"The day of the woman's conference, why didn't you have
on the dress that I gave you the money to buy?" I asked.

"I wasn't able to purchase it. I didn't have any money" she replied.

"I sent you the money when I got paid along with my tithes and offerings" I responded.

"No, you didn't. I didn't receive anything" she said.

"Are you sure? I sent the money and I made sure to notate everything like you said?" I said.

"Yes, I'm positive" she said.

Now, I know I wasn't crazy. I know for a fact that I sent her the $60, with a note on the side stating what it was for. I checked my PayPal account just to make sure. It showed that I did send it and she received it. While checking my PayPal account, she called me.

"Hey, you know what you did send it to me. I'm sorry I didn't see it, I thought that was combined with your tithes and offerings" she said.

"Yes, it was combined altogether. Remember you told me to notate everything, so that you wouldn't get anything mixed up. That's what I did" I said.

"I'm sorry baby girl, it's been so much going on that I didn't even pay attention. If I had known, I would've brought the dress. You saw how I was feeling on that day of the woman's conference. I really didn't know, I'm sorry" she explained.

"It's alright. I just really wanted you to look and feel comfortable. When I didn't see you in the dress, I was confused. It's alright, no worries" I said.

"You know something, when my husband gets in from work. We will bring you your $60. I will give it back because I know how people can get over their money. I just don't want any problems neither do I want to stir up any confusion" she said.

Now, when she said that, she threw me completely off. I wasn't asking her about the dress to get my money back. I was asking because I wanted to know why she didn't have the dress on.

"What exactly do you mean when you say you know how people can get with their money?" I asked.

"What I mean is people will act funny over or with their money. It's alright baby girl you will have it right back as soon as my husband get here" she said.

"Wait a minute…I never asked you for the money back and I have never been one to act funny over some money. I asked about the dress because I notice that you didn't have it on. You said you didn't know I sent the money, that's fine. I am not asking for anything back, if you didn't know…you just didn't know" I explained.

"I understand. I just don't want it to be any problems, so I will still return it" she said.

"There is no problem. I will not accept the money back because that was not my intentions. I just wanted to know and so I asked" I said.

"I just figured it was a problem because you're asking about it?" she said

"No. There is no problem. I was just curious, that's all" I said.

"I apologize again. Next time I will be sure to pay close attention. Go ahead and get you some rest. I will see you tomorrow. I Love You" she said.

"Ok" I responded.

"Why do she always flip the script and play the victim? Why would she assume that I wanted my money back? That whole conversation just threw me completely off. I was better off not even asking her about it" I thought to myself.

All that night I tossed and turned. I did not get any sleep. When I finally was able to fall asleep it was time to get up for prayer and work. My day at work went by so fast. Before I knew it, I was headed to Prophetess Blind house. It was raining hard and traffic wasn't moving fast enough for me. I really believed in my mind that I was going to be late. At this point in my life I was heedless.

I was depleted. All I wanted was to rest in peace for a change. Finally making it through the traffic downtown, headed southbound I realized that I would make it on time. When I arrived at Prophetess Blind house, I went inside her office sat down and watched her as she put on her makeup.

"My husband should be here in a minute. Once he arrives, we will leave out" she said.

"Ok" I responded.

"The other day during Malcolm and Anna's wedding rehearsal, I felt uncomfortable" she said.

"Why? What happened?" I asked.

"Well, his father kept calling me beautiful. He kept offering me things while his mother was right there. I don't

know but I just felt like that was very disrespectful of him"
she said.

"Oh wow! Well maybe that's just the type of guy
Malcolm's father is. That's probably how he greets all
women, not to be disrespectful but to show them respect" I
said.

"Really?! I just believe the only person my husband
should be calling beautiful is me. There are other ways to
show respect. I believe his father was flirting. The crazy
part about all of this is that Malcolm's mother just sat there
and didn't say anything. If it was me, I would've slapped
my husband and told him about himself right then and
there" she said.

"Everyone is different, Like I said that's probably
his father way of showing respect to you and being a
gentleman. I don't think he was flirting. Did you say
something about it? I'm sure if it made you feel
uncomfortable he would've stopped" I said.

"Maybe you're right, but I felt like he was flirting. I
didn't say anything. I figured if Malcolm's mother didn't
address the issue why should I" she said.

"Oh ok. I asked because if I was uncomfortable I
would've said something. I'm sure that whatever may have

been going on could've stopped. Everyone is different though" I said.

While me and Prophetess Blind was talking, Elder Blind walked in.

"Hey! Are you ready to go to this wedding?" he asked.

"Yes. I am" I responded.

"Alright now. As Prophetess Blind armorbearer you need to protect her. Be sure to keep your eyes and ears alert" he said.

"Ok" I responded.

"Is this your first time attending a wedding?" he asked.

"Yes" I said.

"Good! Continue being obedient unto the Lord and your leaders. Before you know it, you will be walking down the aisle and getting married as well" he said.

"Ok" I responded.

"Do you want to get married?" he asked.

"Yes, but not now. I am not ready. There is a lot of things that need to take place within me first" I said.

"Um… ok! Well I can understand that because I wasn't ready either. Before I knew it, I was getting married. So, take your time" he said.

"Alright" I said.

After Elder Blind finished talking, we headed out to Malcolm and Anna's wedding. Since Malcolm didn't stay too far from Prophetess Blind, I decided to just ride with them. Sitting in the backseat, I thought about what Elder Blind said regarding marriage. I didn't have anything against marriage. In fact, I always wanted to get married. However, I never put much thought into it. I just really wanted to get myself together first.

With all the past hurt lingering, unhealthy relationships, and unforgiveness regarding my mother, there was no room in my life for marriage. I was struggling with lust and temptation as well. It was so bad that every time I looked at a man, I automatically pictured myself having sex with him. The temptation was so strong that almost every night before bed, I would sweat bullets, itch and cry for sex. You would think I was in rehab off some sort of drug.

I was at a point in my life where I didn't even want to look at or be around a man. I knew just how messed up and sick in the head, I was as a woman. I didn't want to look at my future husband as a piece of meat. I didn't want my future husband to have to deal with me or try to fill voids that only God can fill. I was a part of this ministry for two years and one month now. It seems as if everything that I thought would get better only got worse.

Malcolm and Anna's wedding was so beautiful. Their wedding theme colors were cream and gold. I believe his mother did the decorating. Malcolm's mother was a beautiful talented woman. She knew how to dress and decorate anything. Their wedding was held inside his mother's house. However, from the looks you would've thought it was in a hall or something just by the set up.

Although this was my first time attending a wedding, deep down something didn't feel right. After the wedding, I was so glad it was over and done with. I felt relieved in a way but drained in every other way. I had one last thing to do and that was to make the announcement about the move.

The following week before Thanksgiving, I spent all my time trying to find more apartments in North Carolina. I wanted to at least have 5 different apartments to choose from. This was the most awkward thing I think I ever had to do. I was unable to find anything and neither did I have any luck with finding a job. Everything started to get even more stressful for me.

I was always in the house unless I had to go to work. Prophetess Blind stated that she didn't want me to get distracted during the process of the move. Although I agreed with her, I never really understood why I couldn't talk to anyone, go out to my work events or just go out in general. If this move is truly the Will of God, nothing can stop, distract or come between that no matter what. As time went on, I begin to talk to Diana more through Facebook messenger.

She helped me out a lot by sending me different work-at-home job links. There was something about Diana that seemed suspicious to me. I couldn't figure it out, but something didn't sit well with me regarding her. As time went on, we only discussed apartments and jobs. She would sometimes talk about different things regarding North Carolina. I didn't trust her enough to talk about anything else. One day after work once I made it home, Prophetess Blind called me.

"Hey baby girl, how was your day?" she said.

"Hey! It was alright and yours?" I said.

"It was good. So how is the apartment search going so far? Have you spoken to Diana?" she asked.

"It's going pretty good. I still haven't found any other apartments though. I was trying to find at least 5 to be able to weigh my options. I spoke to Diana not too long ago. She has been consistent with sending me job links. I have been filling out applications. I still haven't heard back from anyone just yet" I explained.

"Oh wow! Ok sounds good. It's amazing how Diana is consistent in sending you job links and apartments. I haven't heard anything from her regarding finding me a house" she said sarcastically.

"Oh! She's searching for you a house in North Carolina?" I asked.

"Yes. As my armorbearer she will be…well she is supposed to be searching for me a house, but I haven't heard anything from her" she said.

"Oh wow! I didn't know that. She's been busy because it took her awhile to get back to me. Just give her time" I said.

"Shamika, Diana does what she wants to do, when she wants to do it. Once again, when it's regarding her job, school, and family she gets it done. When it comes to this ministry, everything always has to wait. This explains why I called you. I wanted you to start searching for different houses for me and my family. You seem to be on top of this apartment search very well. I know that I can trust you to find me something. Waiting for Diana, it will never get done" she said.

"Ok, I'm not sure how I am going to search for me and you both places to stay but I will try my best. How many bedrooms and bathrooms are you looking to have? What is your budget as far as rent?" I asked.

"See! That's the type of attitude to have when your leader asks you to do something! You didn't complain or anything, instead you are willing to make a way. Therefore, God is going to continuously bless you baby girl! When you take care of your leader, God will take care of you" she said.

Listening to Prophetess Blind, I wondered would it have been the same feedback if I wasn't able to search for her a house. At this point in my life, I didn't know if this was God's Will or her Will. It was starting to seem like she was on a mission to build her own kingdom. I still wasn't quite sure what was going on. If I was sure, I don't think I would be strong enough to say anything. She was too good at playing the victim in any situation.

"It's not a problem, Pastor. How many bedrooms and bathrooms are you looking to have and what's your budget as far as rent?" I asked again.

"I need at least 4 bedrooms with 2 bathrooms and a full basement. Make sure there is a master's bedroom and bathroom. My husband and I can only afford $800 for rent maybe $875 but nothing more. If you can find something below $800 a month that will be perfect" she said.

"Ok, well let me get to it. I will send you an email of every house I find" I said.

"Alright baby girl! Thank You, I Love You" she said.
"Ok" I responded.

"There is no way in this world I am going to find a 4-bedroom 2-bathroom house with a basement for $875 or less. That's impossible! Now I can understand why Diana probably slowly backed out of this situation. This just adds more stress to this whole move thing. I couldn't have told her no because than I would've had to deal with her throwing a tantrum (sigh) Jesus help me!" I said to myself.

For the rest of the week, all I was doing was searching for apartments, houses and jobs in North Carolina. If I wasn't doing that I was at work, on the prayer line and somewhere spending my last dime and food stamp on Prophetess Blind every need. I had no time for nothing but this ministry. I rarely spent time with God, myself or my boys. Thursday came around and I had one more week to make the announcement about the move. Prophetess Blind called at around 7pm, while I was up searching for her a house and more apartments for me.

"Hey Shamika! Are you ready?" she said.

"Ready for what?" I asked confused.

"Remember I said that we were going to start counseling on Thursdays at 7pm for one hour until prayer at 8pm" she explained.

"Oh! Yes! I'm sorry, I forgot" I said.

"Is now an appropriate time? Do you want to start next week?" she asked.

"No. now is good!" I responded.

Although now wasn't a perfect time, once again I didn't want to do anything to irritate her.

"So, tell me what type of woman is your mother?" she asked.

"This counseling is supposed to be for me. Why is she always so interested in my mom?" I thought to myself.

"My mom is a hardworking woman. She is very stubborn and overprotective. However, she is very sweet and caring. If she doesn't know how to do nothing else, she knows how to provide. I had everything I asked for growing up all except her love and undivided attention. She told me she loves me and gave me a kiss, once when I was

7years old. I never heard her say those words to me after that day. Whenever I tried to hug or kiss her she would get infuriated and threaten me. After a while, I just stopped trying. She isn't good at communicating. Any time I asked her about something, she would yell at me. I was always stupid for every decision I made. She would always say what she told me not to do yet she never talked to me about anything" I explained.

"Wow! Ok, I have another question for you. When your mother did and said these things to you... after a while, did she ever apologize?" she asked.

"No. My mom never apologized for anything. I believe her way of saying "sorry" was going out and buying me materialistic things" I said.

"Umm...have you ever heard of something called Love Language?" she asked.

"No. What's that?" I asked.

"Sometimes parents have a challenging time telling their kids they love them. They use different languages. For an example, your mom love language was buying you materialistic things. This is how she showed her love towards you. A love language can be a good thing depending on how it's used. However, it can also throw a sign of confusion to the receiver, which is how you've been feeling all these years" she explained.

"Wow! I didn't know that" I responded.

"Did you finish writing the letter to your mom that I asked you to write?" she asked.

"No. I haven't even started" I said.

"Shamika, I know it hurts and I know it's hard. It's time to let all of this go and forgive your mother" she said.

"I know but I just don't know where to start. Neither do I know what to say without being so harsh" I explained.

"I understand. Just write how you feel and don't leave anything out" she said.

"Ok" I responded.

"Before I go, I just want to say this; Your mother loves you Shamika. Try to understand that this is her way of showing you. I know it hurts because you want her to express her love to you, but she doesn't know how. How is your mother and your grandmother relationship?" she said.

"To be honest, I don't even think they have a relationship. If my mom ever needed anything, I know for a fact my grandma would give it to her" I said.

"You see what I'm saying? Your mother is doing what she has been taught by actions to do. She probably never heard or felt any type of love from your grandmother. The fact that your grandmother was a great provider, that was a sign of love to your mother. Instead of your mother breaking what seems to be a generational curse, she repeated it. However, this curse will be broken by you" she said.

"What do you mean?" I asked.

"Look at how you are with your boys. You don't just show them you love them, but you express it to them as well. You're very active in their life. You're always communicating with them about everything. Instead of repeating how your mother did you, you learned from it. You refuse to treat and allow your boys to feel the same way that you did" she said.

"That's true. I don't ever want my babies to feel that way. If I was to lack in anything as a mother it will never be me rejecting, not loving or giving my boys my undivided attention. By me doing this, doesn't that mean I have forgiven her?" I said.

"Not exactly. The only reason you are this way with your babies is because you can't stand the way it makes you feel. However, just because you are treating them different from how your mother did you, doesn't mean you have forgiven her. You are still looking for an explanation as to way she did you the way she did. Shamika, your mother is never going to give you an answer for her actions. She doesn't even know why herself" she explained.

Listening to Prophetess Blind say these things, I silently cried on the phone. I couldn't understand for the life of me how can a mother not know the pain she has caused her child. When I did even the smallest things to my babies, I always calmed myself down and apologized for my actions. This was just unacceptable and there is no good excuse as to why she did what she did to me.

All I wanted to know was why she treated me the way she did. If it was me or something that I ever did to her, I would apologize and let it all go but I wanted answers. Talking about this situation only made me even more furious and emotional on the inside. This is why, I explained to Prophetess Blind that I would rather leave this alone. Every time I think about it, I hate my mother even more. I really didn't want to feel that way about her, but it was so hard not to. There was a moment of silence on the phone.

"Shamika! Hello? you still there?" she asked.

"Yes, I'm here. It's a bit passed 8, I will talk to you later. I'm about to get on the prayer line" I said.

"Ok, baby girl. I love you! Good night" she said.

"Good night" I responded.

Prophetess Blind has been telling me she loves me since the day she first met me. I wish that I could've said it back and meant it the way she did. I really didn't know what love was. If my own mother didn't even love me, who could possibly take her place and love me. That night, I decided not to get on the prayer line. Instead, I grabbed my notebook and pen. I cried as I begin to write a letter to my mother.

Ma,

I really don't know what to say. To be honest, I don't know what's the point in doing this because you won't care anyway. I care though. I just want to get somethings.......a lot of things off my chest regarding you. It's hurting me so bad. As bad as I don't want to, I hate you and I blame you for everything that ever took place in my life. From the time you put me out when I was only 15 yrs. old to all the many times you came home from work and made me suffer. I made sure everything was the way you wanted it to be. I just wanted to see you smile. All I ever wanted was to have a conversation with you and hear you tell me how beautiful I was and how much you love me. Up until this day, I walk around beat down with the lowest of low self-esteem ever. Everything I ever did was never enough. I was always stupid in your eyes. I was so lost as I learned everything on my own. Every time I failed, here you come telling me what you told me not to do but you never told me nothing. Even when I tried to ask

*questions about certain things, you ignored me and told me I don't
need to know it. But Why? Why did you come home from work that
day and call me a bitch? Why did you put me and my baby out in the
cold? Why didn't you let me dress my son the way I wanted to? That's
my son! not yours! It's not my fault that God didn't bless you with a
son. Every time I dressed a certain way or did my hair a certain way,
why did you always tell me I never looked right? When I graduated,
you didn't even say congratulations. When I brought home good
grades, you didn't even care. I couldn't go anywhere, have company
or even talk on the phone. Hell! I couldn't even look out the window.
All you wanted me to do was stay in my room and make sure your
house was clean but even with me doing just that, you still made me
suffer. I was still your target but Why? What have I ever done to you?
Maybe it's me, maybe I've done something to you that I'm unaware
of. Just tell me, all I ever wanted was a relationship with you. I just
wish I can love you and be loved by you. I blame you for the situation
with Dre and Karter. That's right! I blame you! If only you had loved
me and talked to me about life and what it comes with, I would've
never ran to these men looking for love and seeking attention. I
would've never got pregnant if you wouldn't have put me out. What
did I ever do to you? Don't tell me you don't know why, or you didn't
know how to be there. I didn't know a lot of things, but I know better
than to ever treat my babies the way you did me. I hate you so much
all because you don't love me. Forget everything you ever brought
me, all that materialistic stuff doesn't matter, it never did...it never
will. You being a great provider will never be enough, that meant
nothing to me. Oh God! It hurt so bad! I can't stop crying......Ma,
Please! All I want is your love and attention. I just want you to be
happy for me for a change and stop treating me like a stranger off the
street. I just want to forgive you and let it all go.*

After writing the letter, I placed it inside an envelope. I stored it in a sacred place until it was time to give it to Prophetess Blind. Before bed, I cried out to God.

"Oh God! I just want to let it all go, Please! I just want to forgive her. Father God, can you love me? Can you show me how to love myself and others? Can you show me how love should be and feel? Can you...Please!?" I prayed.

Look upon me with love; teach me your decrees.
-Psalms 119:135 NLT

Before I knew it, Sunday came around quick. Thanksgiving was this upcoming Thursday. I was excited about finally being able to make the announcement. Headed to service, I was perturbed. I never knew what to expect during armorbearer training.

Most of the time spent was used by Prophetess Blind venting. I guess that was a part of training. I listened to her go on and on about someone in the ministry, her car, money and whatever else broke down in her home. As I listened she would always say;

"I just want you to know I am not talking about anyone. I am just venting and it's alright for pastors to vent. We go through as well."

Now I knew the difference between venting and gossiping. She certainly wasn't venting. It had gotten so bad that I would always question myself, wondering was she talking about me as well. Every Sunday, I was beginning to realize that Elder Blind would preach the Word of God regarding whatever Prophetess Blind would be complaining about throughout the week.

Elder Blind preached with so much pride that it was ghastly. If you disagreed with what he was preaching, it didn't bother him at all to tell you to leave. He felt that if you are disagreeing with what he is saying, you're disagreeing with the Word of God. It was confusing because here I am listening to Prophetess Blind complain everyday about numerous things she didn't like. Then on Sundays, it's like Elder Blind, searched scripture to fit what they both wanted verses what God was really saying.

Driving home, I thought about how I gave Prophetess Blind the letter that I wrote to my mom. She didn't read it or anything, she just put it to the side. I wondered what she was going to do with it. Before I could think more about it, my phone rung. It was Prophetess Blind.

"Hello" I said.

"Hey, baby girl! Are you almost home?" she asked.

"Hey! Not yet, just about though. Is everything alright?" I said.

"Oh ok. Yes, everything is fine. I called because I wanted to tell you that now is the time to start saving for the move. Do you have anything put up towards the move?" she said.

"No, I don't. I'm not good with saving at all. I tried it a couple of times, it didn't work" I responded.

"Well baby girl, you are going to have to gain self-control and train yourself. You need to have something set aside. If you do start this process, how much do you think you will be able to save a month?" she said.

Now listening to Prophetess Blind, I immediately got frustrated and even more confused. She waits 4 months before the move to tell me that I need to save. This would have been a great idea, when she first discussed the move with me. However, now just wasn't a valuable time.

"How can I explain this to her without her throwing a tantrum" I thought to myself.

"Hello" she said.

"Yes, I'm here. I have you on speaker while I'm driving, so that's why it sounds like I'm not here" I said.

"Oh ok. So how much do you think you can save a month?" she asked again.

"Pastor, to be honest I don't have any extra money to set aside. This is just not a good time" I said.

"Shamika, are you telling me No?" she asked.

"No, I'm telling you that now is not a good time. I am not good with saving" I said.

"Let me ask you something, do you think God would've placed this on my heart to bring to you, if he knew you wasn't able to do it? And what are you doing with your money that's causing you to not have any extra money? You see, I am going to have to seek God about starting a financial managing bible study session" she said.

"Is she serious right now? I don't have any money because every time I look up she's strategizing my whole check. If it's not her throwing a tantrum, she puts God in the situation. It's like every time I have an opinion, it doesn't matter. It's all about what she wants" I thought to myself.

"You there? You keep getting quiet on me. What are your thoughts?" she said.

"Yes, I'm here. You're right, I guess I can save" I said.

"Are you sure? Just a minute ago you were going through a thing" she laughed.

"Yes, I'm sure" I responded.

"Ok, so about how much can you put aside a month?" she asked.

"$25" I said.

"Shamika, I didn't say every 2 weeks. I said a month" she said.

"I know, and I said $25. That's all I could afford right now" I said.

"Shamika, why do you give me a tough time? That will not be enough. Listen, I will help you. Get you a prepaid visa card and every 2 weeks put $25 on it. Do not spend it. You can spend a little once you have saved 6 months' worth" she explained.

"Ok" I said.

"When you get home look into the visa prepaid cards. When do you think will be an appropriate time to start?" she asked.

"Definitely not this month, I can start the next time I get paid in December" I said.

"That's what I was thinking because we are just about done with November. Are you ready to make the announcement?" she said.

"Yes, I am ready to get it over with" I responded.

"Ok. Just remember, there will be a lot of backlash but stay focused. You are doing the Will of God. A lot of people will not understand that especially since they are not doing his will" she said.

"Ok" I said

"Alright baby girl, talk to you soon" she said.

By the time I got off the phone with Prophetess Blind, I was already home, safe and sound. After kissing my boys' goodnight, I showered and started searching for different prepaid cards. I came across an American Express prepaid card, that I liked so I decided to order it. I also ordered me a rush card as well.

Chapter Seven

I looked up and before I knew it... it was Wednesday, the day before Thanksgiving. I decided to create a group on Facebook messenger with just my immediate family. I wasn't really close to my family and I only had a couple of my relatives' number saved in my phone. I was friends with everyone on Facebook though.

I decided to add Miya in the group as well. Although she was angry with me over something that happened 5 years ago, she still was my friend in my heart. I felt that she needed to know. That evening, I was over excited and so I decided to just make the announcement that day.

"Hey Facebook, the time has arrived for me to make a special announcement. I wanted to do it Thanksgiving Day but it's alright. I decided to share it at this moment. Me and my babies will be moving to Greenville, North Carolina in the Spring of 2017 with my church. This will be my first time living outside of Chicago, so I am a bit scared. However, this is the Will of God. I am trusting him because I know he would never lead me astray" I wrote.

After posting this status, I felt so relieved.

"Finally, it's over and done with" I thought to myself.

I made sure I sent this same message in the group that I created. I really didn't understand why Prophetess Blind said there would be a lot of backlash. I was only getting positive feedback from everyone. My family didn't yet respond. That night, I felt so good and my boys were gone with my aunt. I showered, prayed and went to sleep early.

I tossed and turned all night barely getting any sleep. I was unable to get any rest until I saw that it was daylight outside. Although, I felt relieved from making the announcement; me being tortured through the night didn't change. When I got up the next morning, I checked my phone to numerous notifications from Facebook. Opening them up, I seen that one of them was from my mom, she left a comment.

"You are a weak individual. You will never be nothing more than that. Stop calling my family asking them for help and money to support you and your boys. Ask your pastor for help. You will never be nothing. You will never be strong" she wrote.

After reading this comment, I deleted it while tears were storming from my eyes. It was one thing knowing that my mother didn't care for me based off by her actions. To read over these words she wrote, added to the pain that lingered. I needed someone to talk to so bad. All I had was Prophetess Blind. Picking up my phone I called her while crying uncontrollably.

"Hello" she said.

I burst out crying even more by the sound of her voice.

"It's alright baby girl. Didn't I express to you that you would receive backlash?" she said.

"Yes, but I didn't think it would be anything like this" I responded.

"Well baby girl, I'm sorry to be the one to have to say this but there is more. It's not over yet. The enemy does not want you to do the Will of God. He is going to try his best to stop you from every direction" she said.

While crying, it dawned on me that Prophetess Blind knew exactly what I was crying for when I called.

"How did she know what I was crying about? I could've been crying for numerous reasons. You know what maybe she seen the comment before I did" I thought to myself.

"Are you still there?" she asked.

"Yes. I'm here. I'm just trying to pull myself together. So where is this other backlash going to come from?" I asked.

"You will see. Just remember what I said. The enemy will try to hold you back. Keep being obedient unto the lord" she said.

"Ok" I said.

"Question: Did you receive your prepaid card to start your savings?" she asked.

"Not yet, I was looking at different ones. I decided to order the American express prepaid card. I still ordered a rush card as well" I responded.

"Do you know that certain stores won't accept American express?" she asked.

"Yes, I'm aware of that. Which is perfect because I won't be curious to spend. I chose this card because the fee is $1 a month compared to $5 and up" I said.

"Shamika" she said.

"Yea." I responded.

"I am just trying to help you. I think you should use the rush card. It's a visa and you can use it anywhere. You won't have that option with the America Express card" she explained.

"I understand. I remember you saying that I wouldn't be able to spend the money until after six months. I just figured since I won't be really using it, it wouldn't really matter. I will just take money off at an ATM if anything" I said.

"Shamika, baby girl…use the rush card for your savings. You can use the other card for your own personal savings for something else, like your house needs or something" she said.

"Ok" I said.

I am not sure why it was a big deal about which card I would be using to save. Prophetess Blind seemed a bit frustrated about it. I decided to just use me the rush card to make her feel better. After receiving the rush card, I called Prophetess Blind to let her know.

"Hello" I said.

"Hey baby girl, what's going on?" she said.

"Hey, I was just calling to see when I should start saving. I received my rush card and set everything up so that the money would be automatically transferred over" I explained.

"Ok, good. Now here is the thing, I just want to help you and make sure you pull all the way through with your savings" she said.

"Ok, so when should I start?" I asked again.

"Shamika, I need you to give me the card. I will hold it for you until June 2017, which will be 6 months from now. I will give it back so that you can purchase whatever you want" she said.

"Ok, but can you explain to me how this is teaching me how to gain self-control financially?" I asked.

"You won't be tempted to spend it, if you don't have access to it" she said.

"Ok, I will give you the card Sunday before service" I said.

"Shamika, I need full access to the card which means the account setup as well. I am just trying to help you. It's one thing for me to have the card but you're still able to shop online. If you have any type of access to the card, you will be tempted to use it" she said.

"Ok and that's where self-control comes in at. Now I'm confused" I said.

"That's only because you want to do what you want to do and that's not going to help you save anything. I know all of this may sound crazy but once again, I am just trying to help" she said.

"Ok" I said.

This whole saving and me giving her my card with full access to my account idea, just didn't sit well with me. I felt suspicious about it. When Sunday came around, I arrived early as usual for armorbearer training. I gave Prophetess Blind my card, but she didn't have my account information. I just didn't feel right about that. Once I sat down and got settled, Prophetess Blind sat at her desk and looked directly at me.

"Someone in this ministry is going to try to break off and do their own thing but it's not going to work. However, they will realize when they choose to be disobedient unto the lord, there will be consequences" she said.

As she spoke these words I wondered who she could be talking about. It was only 6 people a part of the ministry and that's including me. Instead of wondering I decided to ask.

"Who would do something like that? Diana and Terry maybe? Because I know you are always complaining about them" I said.

"No, not them" she said.

"Malcom and Anna…Tia?" I asked.

"No, not them either?" she said.

"Well that only leaves me…is it me?" I asked.

"Girl no, it's not you!" she laughed.

"Aw ok, well that's just about everyone, so who could it possibly be then?" I asked.

"You will see but let's get started" she said.

"Ok" I responded.

"Oh wait! Have you spoken to your mother after all that backlash?" she asked.

"No. I have nothing to say to her. I'm done with her. She has always spoken negative to me and towards anything I have ever did in my life. That's it! I'm done!" I responded.

"I understand, baby girl. I was going to tell you that you should block her. Once we all move and get settled in North Carolina, then you can unblock her. I just don't want her to keep coming with the negative comments trying to discourage you from moving" she said.

Listening to Prophetess Blind tell me to block my mom ached my soul. I know my mom never seem to have anything positive to say. However, I loved her too much to block her out. We always had our disagreements, but I never took it that far as to block her. We got into it more than usual, but we still always find ourselves back to one another. That was my mom at the end of the day.

"So, what are your thoughts about blocking her" she asked.

"I mean…I don't think it's that serious. I maybe angry with her but that's still my babies' grandma. I don't want them to suffer because of a choice I decided to make. I don't understand… if this whole move thing is the Will of God, I don't think anything can stop or come between what he called me to do" I explained.

"Shamika, I am just trying to help. I think that would be an innovative idea. Look at how your mom feels about you. Her motives are not right when it comes to you. Sometimes we all need to just distance ourselves from certain situations and people who means us no good. Since this is the case, I think that you should. This is the Will of God for us all to move. The enemy is busy, he will use any and everything to distract you. I just want you to be careful and remain focus, that's all" she said.

"You're right. I will block her" I said.

I really didn't understand why I had to block my mom, yet I did it anyway. Although lately everything she has been doing and saying seemed suspicious, my surety was with Prophetess Blind.

"Well baby girl, it looks like we ran a bit overtime. It's already time for service. We will pick back up with training next week" she said.

"Ok" I said.

While walking out of her office into the living room she stopped me.

"How is the apartment searching going for you? Were you able to find any houses around that price range?" she asked.

"It's a bit stressful. No, I can't find any houses at that price range in Greenville. I've been seeing a lot of cheap houses near Greensboro, Rocky Mount and Goldsboro. I know you stated only in Greenville, so I disregarded those" I explained.

"You know something I spoke to Diana not long ago. She stated that it's small in North Carolina. She stated that all the cities are less than 30 minutes away from one another. If you see any more houses in those cities that's fine, since it's not that far from Greenville" she said.

"Are you sure?" I asked.

"Yes, Its fine. What about you? Where you able to find at least 4 more apartments to choose from?" she asked.

"No. I still haven't had any luck with that" I said.

"Ok, well don't worry about it, just keep searching for the houses. Remember what I said; when you take care of your leader, God will provide for you" she said.

"Ok" I said.

Service started and just like every other Sunday, Elder Blind preached God's word with so much pride. I'm not quite sure but maybe that's how it was supposed to be. The time was getting closer and closer for me to finally move. Each day I was doing nothing more than searching for a place to stay at a reasonable price. It was hard for me because I couldn't find anything.

Every time, I would explain this to Prophetess Blind, she would always say just search for her house and God will take care of me. As I was searching for houses for her, I found a couple and emailed them to her. It seemed as if she still wasn't satisfied.

"Hey baby girl, how are you?" she said.

"I'm alright and you?" I said.

"I'm good actually. I wanted to talk about these houses you have been emailing me" she said.

"Ok" I responded.

"Now here is the thing, most of these houses require a credit check. Me and my husband is going through bankruptcy now, which means we are trying to stay away from any credit checks. If you can, while searching call around and see if you can speak with the landlord. It would be great for us if they can take cash payments up front" she said.

"It's like every time she tells me to do one thing something always goes wrong. She just keeps adding more to what I already have" I thought to myself.
"You there?" she asked.

"Yes, I'm here. I'm just listening, so you want me to call around and talk to landlords in the mist of searching for houses?" I said.

"Yes, would that be too much for you to do?" she asked.

"No" I said.

"Ok. Also, have you been looking around for movers as well?" she asked.

"No. I decided to just fly there and start all over again. I wanted to buy everything new once I moved" I said.

"Oh ok, so what are you going to do with all your stuff? she asked.

"I am going to give it all away. Whoever want it, can have it" I said.

"Wow! Even your TVs and bedroom sets? That stuff is still in good condition. It's as good as new. Are you sure?" she asked.

"Yes, I'm sure. I just want to start fresh. I don't want to take anything with us" I said.

"Can I have it? Especially your furniture. This way I won't have to worry about anything once I move. Hopefully, me and my husband will only have enough to move and pay the rent down there. We won't be able to buy things for the house until later down the line" she said.

"Yes, you can have it" I said.

"God is going to bless you, baby girl. Whenever you have some free time on your hands, investigate different moving companies and see what's their prices. Be sure to let me know" she said.

"Ok" I responded.

The following week I searched for more houses and called around to different moving companies. To move all of Prophetess Blind belongings including the stuff that I was giving her, was a total of $3,058.00. Although it was a lot of things she told me to get done, I always managed to get everything done. I emailed her 5 more houses that didn't require a credit check and they all was within her budget.

At this point, I was just waiting on her to respond. I was hoping that she wouldn't complain or throw a tantrum. One day while at work on my break, I decided to check my Facebook page. My aunt Renee left a comment on my post I made about the announcement.

"God is Love" she said.

"Ok" I replied.

"God is Love….and he would never tell you to block out your family, especially your mother" she said.

"Well she shouldn't always have something negative to say about everything I do" I replied.

"God is Love….and he will never harm you, mislead you or force you to do anything. Seek and listen to only him! Let him lead you!" she said.

"Ok" I replied.

I logged off Facebook and headed back to work. On my way home after work, Renee called me.

"Hello" I said.

"Can you just tell me when you are leaving?" she asked.

"I am leaving in the Spring of 2017, no later than April" I said.

"I really don't feel right about this Shamika. I really don't. I don't want you to think I'm trying to hold you back. You really need to think this out. I really believe this is something your pastor is coming up with, not God" she said.

"This is God's Will, I know it is" I said.

"Shamika, listen I think you done got wrapped up in something that's not good and its controlling you. I had a dream that you were somewhere trapped far away, and you called your mom to come get you. I don't think you should leave" she explained.

"I have to go and do the Will of God. I will be fine and the last person I will be calling is my mom" I said.

"Ok" she said.

When I got off the phone, I pulled over and thought about everything Renee said. I cried thinking back to the many dreams I had after having a conversation with Prophetess Blind. Every time she told me not to do something, I would toss and turn that very night with torturing dreams. I would then get up and do whatever she told me to do without seeking God about it first.

"What if Renee was right? What if Prophetess Blind was the enemy trying to keep me away from God?" I thought to myself.

I sat in my car for 20 minutes crying out to God,

"Jesus! What's going on? Am I being deceived? Am I being used and mislead? Why won't you answer me?! Please! I'm so tired of feeling this way! I'm so tired of crying! I can't even sleep! I can't sleep! I can't sleep! I can't sleep! Father, all I ask is that if I'm being deceived, please help me and set me free" I cried.

Once I made it in, I realized I had a lot of time to spare. I decided to take a nap before I headed out to get my babies. While laying down my phone rung. It was Prophetess Blind.

"I don't want to talk to her right now" I said to myself.

I throw my phone down and laid back down only for it to ring again, it was my dad. I answered.

"Hello" I said.

"What's going witchu baby? Why I ain't heard from you? How my grandbabies doing?" he asked.

"Nothing much, just working. They're doing good" I responded.

"Aw ok…ok. Why you sound all dead and shit? You sound all down and out" he said.

"I don't know. I didn't know I sounded like that but I'm alright" I said.

"You a damn lie and if don't nobody else know you…yo daddy do. I know some wrong. I hear it in yo voice" he said.

"What is you talking about? I'm serious, I'm alright" I laughed.

"um hmm…whatever. So, what's this about you moving to North Carolina stuff on Facebook? What's up with that?" he asked.

"Me and the boys are moving with my church in March or April next year" I said.

"Ok so why am I just now hearing about this and why do y'all have to move?" he asked.

"I'm sorry. I should've told you sooner than now and my pastor says it's the Will of God" I said.

"Shamika, listen you know I'm with you no matter what. Whatever you ever wanted to do, it was cool with me but baby this right here…something just ain't right. I'm not feeling this one" he said.

"Here you go! I never thought I would be hearing you say something like this. You sound just like everybody else with all this negativity" I said.

"What the fuck you mean here I go? Shamika, how long have you known this pastor of yours? How long have you and my grandbabies been a part of this church? And what you mean your pastor said it's the Will of God? So, you mean to tell me it's not his Will for you to stay here and praise him and continue on having a relationship with him?" he asked.

"I've been a part of this church for 2 going on 3 years. I trust my pastor. I know she would never lead me wrong or tell me to do something that's not of God" I said.

"Ok, I understand the respect that you have for your pastor but if she wants to move than let her go. Shamika, you barely even know these people. 2 going on 3 years…shid you just beginning to know them if you ask me. It takes about 2 to 3 years to get to know anybody in any kind of relationship period. Shamika listen, you scaring the hell outta me, man. This shit ain't right! I don't give a fuck what nobody talking about, this shit ain't right. You just don't up and move far away with people you barely know. Whoever your pastor is she need her ass beat for having you think that you have to do something like this. Shamika, do your daddy a favor. Think about this shit because it doesn't make sense" he said.

"Ok" I responded.

"I'm serious!" he yelled.

"I am too. Even though my mind is made, I will think over everything" I said.

"Alright, yo daddy love you baby. Tell my grandbabies I love'em. Talk to you later" he said.

"Ok" I said.

When I got off the phone with my daddy, our whole conversation replayed in my mind. This was the first time in my life that my daddy was not on my side. I was beginning to think that something was wrong with this whole move thing. No matter what, my daddy always was honest and straightforward with me about everything.

My dad was my best friend. I didn't grow up with him living under the same roof as me. However, that didn't stop him from being a part of my life. I was the oldest out of 6 kids on my father's side. Although my relationship with my mom wasn't the best, my relationship with my dad was everything and more.

Growing up, I was able to talk to my dad about everything. He shared a lot with me as well and we never sugar-coated anything for one another, right or wrong. He has always been consistent and supportive in my life. He never missed a birthday, holiday, graduation or any other special life events regarding me. He never played favoritism when it came to me.

Although he basically stated the same thing as Renee, I honored what he had to say. Laying in silence, I thought about everything everyone had been saying to me regarding Prophetess Blind. Tears flowed from my eyes as every word she ever preached replayed in my mind. Lately she had been preaching one thing but doing another.

Her complaints turned into sermons preached by Elder Blind on Sundays. It was as if they only applied the word of God when it was beneficial for them. I was starting to believe that they used God for their own selfish reasons to keep everyone apart of the ministry where they wanted us to be.

While thinking to myself, my phone began to ring. It was Prophetess Blind again, I decided not to answer. She was either calling me regarding some money or to tell me what God said not to do. I just didn't have time. My phone beeped, she texted me:

"Hey baby girl, I am hoping all is well. Do not let all the backlash get the best of you. I have something that I wanted to share with you. Give me a call when you get a chance."

I made up in my mind that I would call her back if not tomorrow the day after. It's not that I didn't want to talk to anyone, I just didn't want to talk to her. My phone rang again, this time it was my sister Samantha.

"Hello" I said.

"Hey, can I come over and spend Christmas with you and the boys?" she asked.

"Hey, Yes! That's cool. I don't have any money now. I won't be able to get you anything until after Christmas" I said.

"That's ok. Mommy and my dad got me something. Mommy, brought you and the boys something as well" she said.

"Ok. I will pick you up. It will probably be when I get off work Christmas Day, so be ready" I said.

"Ok" she responded.

I was awestruck that Samantha told me my mom got me something for Christmas. I had forgot all about Christmas and the fact that it was a week away. I even forgot about my birthday which is 3 days before Christmas. My mind was in a million places all circled around this whole moving thing. I forgot about a lot of things and people. I didn't have any friends. All I did was go to work and service. The only person I talked to was Prophetess Blind but all of that was about to stop. Something equivocal was going on. I made up in my mind that I wasn't taking this to anyone but God.

Looking at the time, I realized I only had 45 minutes to go pick up my babies from school. While leaving out, my phone rang again.

"Jesus! if this woman calls me one more time!" I said to myself.

Looking at my phone, it wasn't Prophetess Blind… it was Dre. He was video calling me off Facebook messenger. I was startled so I didn't answer. Once he stopped calling, I wondered to myself what could he have wanted. Walking to my car, Dre video called me again. This time I answered.

"What's up! how you been?" he asked.

"Nothing much. How you been doing?" I said.

"I'm good. I'm in Washington, DC, getting ready for my speech. This the first time I spoke outside of Chicago" he explained.

"Aw ok. Congratulations! Look at you moving on up" I laughed.

"lol you funny. So how you been?" he asked.

"I been alright. Why you keep asking me that?" I said.

"Because I care about you. I just want to make sure that you're alright, for real. I saw that comment your mom left on Facebook too. To be honest with you, I agree with what she said" he said.

"Wow! I can expect this type of response from you Dre, but I really don't have time for this. I just don't want to talk about it" I said.

"Shamika, I just need you to listen to me. I know we haven't talked in a while, but I still care for you. This whole moving thing is just not right. I really believe that you know it's not right. You're just going along with it, like you always do. You never say anything, you always just go with everything. You be quick to block everything and everybody out who don't agree with you. Shamika, you're not always right and neither am I but please hear me out on this one" he said.

"Dre, I am on my way to get my boys. Now is not the time to talk about this" I said.

"Ok, you don't have to talk. Why can't you just drive and listen to what I'm saying?" he asked.

"Because I don't want to hear anything else about this! My mind is made and I'm moving!" I yelled.

"Shamika, do you even know these people?" he asked.

"Yes, I do" I responded.

"Do you know them well enough to be moving away with them" he asked.

"Yes, Dre!" I yelled.

"Ok, why are you yelling? I'm talking to you in a calm way and you should do the same" he said.

"Ok, I have to go" I said.

"See now you pissing me the fuck off! Every time I try to talk to you about anything all you wanna do is run from the situation and act like everything ok. But it's not! It's not Shamika! This shit not right! And you know it!" he yelled.

Tears stormed from his eyes.

"Dre, why are you crying? Listen, it's the Will of God. I will be fine, trust me" I said.

"Because I love you. I just want you to be safe. If it's the Will of God, shouldn't we all be filled with joy and glad to see you go? This is not right! I told my granny about this and she said the same thing. You know when granny say something she's right. Shamika Please! Can you promise me this one thing?" he said.

"What" I asked.

"Can you promise me that you will really sit down and think about this?" he asked.

"Yea" I responded.

"No! promise me" he said.

"I promise that I will think about it, Dre. I can't drive and talk, I have to go" I said.

"Ok, thank you" he said.

Pulling up in front of my babies' school, I sat in my car before I went in. I can't believe Dre called me. Even though, I hadn't talked to him due to the whole situation about David not being his. He would still call me from time to time.

To this day, Dre still struggles with forgiving me for the hurt I've caused him. I can't believe he told granny. Granny was Dre's grandmother. Although me and Dre went our separate ways in life, his whole family still respected me and my babies. Just thinking about everything and everyone I was getting ready to move away from, I got emotional.

Renee, my dad and Dre called and they all stated the same thing. It all summed up what my mom said as well. Dre was right I knew something wasn't right, I felt it. I know when something is going on. Instead of addressing it, I isolate myself and go with the flow.

Anyone with ears to hear should listen and understand.
-Mark 4:23 NLT

Finally, pulling myself together I went inside my boy's school. Instantaneously I ran into Mrs. Eternal.

"Hey Beautiful! Give me a hug" she said.

"Aww baby, God got you in his hands. Do you hear me? You don't have anything to worry about. God got it all figured out. Keep going to him and he will lead you. He'll show you everything you desire to know and more. He is patiently waiting on you to come to him" she said.

"Ok" I said.

"I love you so much! You and those babies. I'm right here if you need me. Have a good night!" she said.

"Ok, you do the same" I said.

That night, I had that same dream again. Diana was yelling at me and behind her Prophetess Blind fell. I was standing in a dark place not knowing what was going on. I begin to cry while Diana kept yelling at me. I woke up sweating and wondering what was that all about. Normally when I dream about something, I don't dream about it twice. For me to have this same dream again, left me tousled.

I stayed awake for a little bit, then I nodded off into another dream. Spiders where everywhere as I walked up these stairs to a house. They were crawling all around me and even hanging from the porch. There were webs everywhere. Nothing touched me as I passed through and opened the door. I woke up by the sound of my alarm, it was time for me to get on the prayer line. While on the prayer line Prophetess Blind seemed to be very upset. After prayer she spoke to us all,

"Listen, I am tired of people and their ways and guess what I don't have to deal with it. I have been nothing but good and people still aren't satisfied. I don't want to be like Moses, see he allowed the people to make him angry with God. This caused him to die before he entered the land he was leading the people of Israel into. I'm not doing that anymore! If people want to do and act however they please then so be it! I am done! If God is not dealing with it then why should I? If you all are fed up as well then I advise you all to get before God" she said.

Every time she spoke, I always wondered who she could be talking about. Everyone that was a part of the ministry was on the prayer line already. She didn't have any friends and all she did was sit in the house. I always felt like she was throwing indirect signals to someone apart of the ministry.

After getting off the prayer line, I started getting ready for work. While driving I had a long talk with God.

"Jesus, continue to show me and keep me in the mist of whatever is going on" I prayed.

Let me hear of your unfailing love each morning, for I am trusting you. Show me where to walk, for I give myself to you.
-Psalms 143:8 NLT

My day at work was a breeze. I was having a wonderful day. It seemed like when I took a day or two from talking to Prophetess Blind, I felt relieved. Headed home from work, my cousin Faith called me.

"Hey Shamika girl! What's going on?" she said.

"Hey Faith! I'm good. How have you been?" I responded.

"Aw girl, I'm good! I was calling because you know it's almost income tax time. I was wondering if you wanted me to do your taxes this year. You know you gone get way more back than you did last year" she said.

"You know something I haven't been thinking about my taxes but yes I want you do them for me this year" I said.

"Girl what you mean you ain't been thinking about it. That's your money" she laughed.

"My mind has been all everywhere lately. When can we start? What do I need again?" I asked.

"Well, December is just about over. Did you receive your last check stub yet? You know I can just use that to get all your information in. This way I can at least give you an estimate of what you're getting back. Now I won't be able to submit it though. I think the date to submit everything is January 24, 2017" she explained.

"Ok that's cool, I get paid tomorrow. Maybe we can meet somewhere and get everything done one day next week" I said.

"Ok, that's cool. What you got planned for your birthday? You know you always get all pretty and step out for your birthday" she laughed.

"Lol, yes I know but this time is different. I'm just not feeling my birthday. I forgot it was approaching, I just don't have the funds to do anything" I explained.

"Yeah, I know how you feel. Well, I will talk to you later" she said.

"Ok" I responded.

Chapter Eight

Whenever I talked to Faith, she never brought up anything that I was dealing with. We always had a normal conversation. If I ever wanted to talk to someone, she would be the first person that I call. I'm not sure if she knew what was going on or not. However, she made room for me to come to her about it, she didn't pressure me.

After getting off the phone with Faith, I decided to call Prophetess Blind.

"Hey, how are you? did you receive the houses?" I asked.

"Hey baby girl! Yes, I received the houses. I like that big white one in Goldsboro, NC. I see its $975 though" she said.

"Yes. That's was the best I could do" I replied.

"Did you try to call the landlord to see if they will accept the rent in cash? Remember I told you me and my husband are going through bankruptcy. We wouldn't be able to let anyone run our credit" she explained.

"I'm sorry but I wasn't able to call the landlord. I sent you the information maybe you should call" I said.

"Yes, I know. I will have Diana call the landlord. She can go look at the house for me since she doesn't stay too far" she said.

"Ok" I responded.

"Did you call around to moving companies to get an estimate?" she asked.

"Yes, I did actually. To move everything and take everything to North Carolina the balance came out to $3,058.00" I explained.

"Wow! That's a lot" she said.

"Yes, I know that's why I said I wasn't taking anything with me. It's too expensive" I said.

"Well God will work it out. After all, this is his Will and so we just have to wait on him" she said.

"Ok" I responded.

"Are you alright? You just don't sound like yourself" she asked.

"To be honest, No! I'm not alright. Everyone is calling me and they all are saying the same thing as far as me moving" I said.

"And what's that?" she asked.

"They are all saying this move is not right and not of God. They are saying that this is something that you came up with. Is that true?" I said.

"Shamika, I explained to you that it would be a lot of backlash. Why would I come up with something like this? Do you honestly believe that I want to leave my family? Do you think I want to live outside of Chicago? I have never been outside of Chicago. I'm nervous as well but I'm trusting God. Therefore, I told you to not talk to anyone because I didn't want you to get distracted and change your mind about the Will of God" she explained.

"I understand all of that but why is it more than one person saying the same thing? I remember you saying that if more than one person is saying the same thing about someone, something isn't right. I'm just trying to get a better of understanding of all of this, that's all" I said.

"Now see… now your twisting what I said to use it for this situation. I taught that lesson in bible study regarding our ways…like our attitude and our pride. This is what happens when you are doing the Will of God. Shamika, the enemy is busy when it comes to you. He does not want you to do the Will of God. There is no in between, you're either in or you're out" she said.

"I'm not trying to twist anything. That's not my intentions. You weren't specific with what it meant around that time. I thought it meant for any and every situation. Ok so, in this situation what does it mean?" I said.

"It doesn't mean nothing. It's a distraction and you're allowing it to hold you back" she laughed.

"Shamika, can I ask you a question?" she said.

"Yeah" I responded.

"How do you feel about the move to North Carolina now that it's getting closer?" she asked.

"I'm not really sure how I feel. I want to do the Will of God but its draining. I haven't been getting any sleep or peace. I am being tortured at night when I dream and I'm just tired. Is this how the Will of God is supposed to be? I'm steady searching for a place to stay and a job but nothing is coming through for me. I listen to you and I try to hold on a little longer, yet it seems as if things are only getting worse. To be honest, I listen to what you preach and then what you turn around and say to me... it's just not adding up. I don't know how to feel right now about anything" I explained.

"Shamika, the dreams are witchcraft. I explained this to you before. You must pray against that witchcraft spirit. What do you mean what I preach and say is not adding up! Do you see what's going on? Do you see how the enemy have your mind in places it shouldn't be? I can't believe you would say something like that to me" she said.

"Why am I even having witchcraft dreams? Where did this stuff come from? I wasn't having them before I met you. Everyone is saying the same thing but you're the only one saying something different. Is this really the Will of God?" I said.

"Hold on a minute …Shamika, I will call you right back. I have to take this call" she said.

"Ok" I responded.

Prophetess Blind never told me she would call me back in the middle of a conversation. Not saying that she can't do that, but it just seemed strange. I wonder was someone on her other line or did she just didn't have the answers to what I was asking. To be honest, I really don't think she cared about anything I was talking about. Something just wasn't right and normally when I feel this way, something isn't right. Waiting for her to call back, I laid in my bed and stared at my ceiling.

"Jesus, am I being deceived? If so, can you show me who it is? Can you strengthen me to remain calm when you do reveal this person to me?" I prayed.

For the remaining of that day, I did not hear back from Prophetess Blind. I didn't bother to call her back to see why. That night, I had a regular dream for the first time in a long time. I dreamed that I was in a waiting room inside of a college. I was holding some papers in my hand, but I couldn't see clearly what they stated. A lady called my name; I got up, walked inside her office and sat down.

"Are you ready for your new classes" the lady asked.

"Yes" I responded.

"Are you sure?" she asked

"Yes, I'm sure" I said.

After responding, I woke up. This time when I woke up I felt relaxed.

"Jesus, do you want me to go back and finish school?" I thought to myself.

Before I knew it, it was Christmas day. By my surprise I didn't have to work. My birthday came and went so fast. I treated it like a normal day. I just wasn't in the birthday spirit. I wasn't in any kind of spirit to be honest. I got up early that morning and started getting ready to go get my sister. I'm not sure if I was more excited to pick her up or see what my mom had got me for Christmas.

Here I am 27 years old and my mom still thinks of me on Christmas. One thing she has never missed was Christmas and my birthday. Even though they were so close together, she still managed to spoil me with gifts. Driving to my mom house I felt so good maybe Prophetess Blind was right. My mother's love language was buying me materialistic things. Although she didn't know how to love me the way I wanted her too, this was her way of loving me.

"Who am I too judge her? That's it! I'm letting this go. I'm seeking God to forgive her. I love my mom too much to hold this against her" I thought to myself.

Arriving at my mom house, I called my sister to come outside. As she walked outside she only had a big bag of toys for my babies. I didn't see anything for me.

"Maybe Samantha lied" I thought to myself.

Once she got settled in the car she dug deep into her pocket and pulled out a small box.

"Here…this is for you from mommy" she said.

"Ok. Sit it right there. I will open it once I make it home" I said.

I was curious to see what it was, but I didn't want to open it while driving. On my way driving home, Renee called me.

"Hey, can the boys spend Christmas day with me? I brought them gifts" she said.

"Yes, I picked up Samantha though. Can she come over too?" I asked.

"Yes, I brought her something too. Bring all of them over" she said.

"Ok. I'm on my way now. I will be to pick them up tomorrow when I get off work" I said.

"Ok" she said.

After dropping off my babies and sister. I rushed back home just to see what my mom brought me. I walked in my house and sat the small box on the kitchen counter. I slowly opened the box to a 14kt white gold chain with a diamond heart pendant.

"OMG!" I yelled.

I knew from this gift that my mother was sorry for what she said. I was so excited that I called Prophetess Blind.

"Hello" she said.

"Merry Christmas! You are not going to believe this" I said.

"Merry Christmas. Is everything alright?" she said.

"Yes! My mom brought me a beautiful chain with a diamond heart pendant for Christmas" I said.

"Wait a minute…What!?" she said.

"Yes! And it's so beautiful. Pastor you were right, this is my mother's way of saying sorry. This is definitely her love language to me" I said.

"I am going to video chat with you off Facebook. I would like to see this chain" she said.

"Ok" I responded.

During the video chat, I held the chain up so that Prophetess Blind could see it.

"Shamika, I don't have a good feeling in me about this chain. It is beautiful though, but your mother's spirit is not right towards you. Looking at this chain reminds me of a story in the bible… It was regarding someone accepting a gift from someone else who didn't like them, and they died" she explained.

"What!" I yelled.

"Shamika, calm down. I know this may sound crazy, but you can't keep the chain. It will harm you if you do" she said.

"What do you mean it will harm me? This is my mother's way of saying she is sorry. We talked about this during therapy…remember?" I said confused.

"Yes, I remember but that was then, this is now. Her spirit is not right towards you" she said.

"Pastor, I'm confused. From my understanding, I have always been a target in my mother eyes. Her spirit has never been right towards me if that's the case. What are you saying right now?" I said.

"Shamika, I am just trying to help you. I'm saying that you can't keep the chain. It will harm you. God is not pleased with this, I can feel it deep within my spirit. You have to get rid of it" she said.

"How?! Ok so what am I supposed to do with it? Give it back to her?" I asked.

"I don't want to tell you what to do with it because I don't want people to say I made them do anything. All I know is that you have to get rid of it" she said.

"What are you talking about you don't want people to say you made them do anything? I'm asking you, since you say I can't keep it…what do you suggest I do with it? I don't want to have any more nightmares and witchcraft dreams that I'm already having. So, if you give me the word to throw it out I will do it" I said.

"Ok, Throw it out. I just want you to be safe" she said.

"Ok, I will throw it out. It's getting late and I'm tired" I said.

"Ok baby girl, I love you" she said.

"Ok" I responded.

Getting off the phone I placed the chain back inside the box. I walked into my room and climbed in my bed.

"Who would ever think I'd be crying on Christmas day? She told me that this was my mother's way of showing me love. Now, she's saying that basically my mother's way of showing me love is going to harm me. Which one is it? I am so confused" I thought silently to myself.

I cried myself into another crazy dream. I dreamed of sitting at this desk in a classroom that was pitch black. The only light that was on was a red light. It was a man writing on the chalkboard with his back turned, I couldn't see his face. I looked to see what he was writing but all his words were backwards. In front of me was a bible and the moment I looked at it, it opened and flipped to the book of Matthew. I begin to read the bible, but the man turned around.

"PAY ATTENTION!" he yelled.

Immediately I closed the bible and looked at the board. I was so afraid because his eyes were black. I got up and ran out of the classroom without looking back. Once I made it out the building, I ran into a maze. While running through this maze full of trees, out of nowhere huge spiders begin to chase me. I heard that man yell "PAY ATTENTION!" again. His voice sounded familiar the second time he said it. It was Prophetess Blind voice.

I hopped up sweating, trying to catch my breath. I looked at the clock and it was midnight. When I got up, I felt reeling as I walked to the kitchen to get a bottled water. I sat down in the kitchen.

"I am not going back to sleep. Could this chain be the reason I just had that dream" I thought to myself.

I checked my Facebook page to see who was active and there was Prophetess Blind. She was always up late nights. She wouldn't go to sleep until after we got off the prayer line at about 4:30am.

"Could Renee be right about Prophetess Blind controlling my dreams? Is that even possible?" I thought to myself.

I decided to call Prophetess Blind and finish our conversation. I realized she never called me back.

"Hello, Hey Pastor" I said.

"Hey Shamika, what are you still doing up?" she asked.

"I couldn't sleep, I had another crazy dream" I said.

"Is that so? Did you throw out that chain yet?" she asked.

"No, not yet" I said.

"Well, that explains this crazy dream that you had" she said.

"Ok. What about all the other dreams before I got this chain?" I asked.

"Shamika, its witchcraft. You have to pray against it" she said.

"From where?! From where?!" I yelled.

"Shamika, calm down. I know exactly how you feel. I've experienced what you're going through. It's through your family bloodline, it's a generational curse. Pray against it and it will go away. Remember, you are going to be the one that break the curse" she said.

"I am praying but it's like it gets worse" I said.

"Well baby girl, it gets worse just before it gets better, so don't stop" she said.

"Ok. What happen to you the other day? I was waiting on you to call me back?" I asked.

"Oh! I'm sorry. I was so busy. Listen I wanted to talk to you about something" she said.

"Ok, what's going on?" I asked.

"Have you ever thought about staying with me when we move to North Carolina? I know you were having trouble finding a place, so I thought to ask. It would be better to stay with me until you get settled enough to find you a place. I talked to God and my husband about it already and they said it's alright" she explained.

There was a moment of silence.

"Hello" she said.

"Yes, I'm here" I responded.

"What do you think about that? I am just trying to help you" she said.

"I appreciate your help but me and my boys really just need our own space" I said.

"Ok, well once again I am just trying to help" she said.

"If this move is God's Will I will find a place no matter what, right?" I asked.

"Yes, that's right but let me get ready for bed. I will talk to you later. Please do not forget to throw out that chain. I just want you to be safe. I Love You, Good night" she said.

"Ok, Good night" I responded.

"Why in the world would she ask me to come and live with her? I would never stay with her. She is nasty, her house stank, and her kids drives me crazy. They half clean the house and none of them do anything right. I be ready to go the moment I get there for service and training. Wait, did she say she asked God and her husband and they both said yes. What in the world is going on?" I said to myself.

I looked at the chain my mother brought me one last time. Something in me did not want to throw it out but I didn't want God to be angry with me. I placed it back in the box and throw it away. I grab all the garbage from around the house and took it out.

"Now maybe I will have some peace" I thought to myself.

While thinking to myself, my phone rung.

"Who is this calling me at 2 in the morning" I said to myself.

I looked at my phone, it was Alex; my coworker.

"Hey Shamika! Can you please work my overnight shift today and I will go in and work your morning shift?" she asked.

"Sure" I responded.

"Ok, I am going to fill out the form for us switching shifts. Please be sure to sign it when you come in tonight and place it on Marie's desk. Thank you so much" she said.

"Ok, no problem" I responded.

Although that was unexpected, I really needed to switch shifts. There was no way I was going to have enough strength to go to work in a couple of hours. I was still afraid to go back to sleep, so I stayed up surfing Facebook.

"Let me unblock Karter and see what he's doing......naw maybe I should leave that alone. I am already dealing with enough stuff as it is. Naw, you know what...imma just see how he doing and that's it" I thought to myself.

I unblocked Karter and messaged him at 2:45am.

"You up?" I asked.

"Yea, what's up?" he replied.

"I miss you. Can you come over here with me?" I asked.

"Where you at?" he asked.

"Home" I replied.

"Ok, I'll be there in about 20 minutes" he said.

"Ok" I replied.

I know I was wrong for reaching out to Karter. If anything, he was supposed to be reaching out to me regarding his son. I didn't like Karter, I just enjoyed having sex with him. The way he flew when I called him for sex, is how I desired for him to come when I called him for his son.

Karter arrived in exactly 20 minutes. That morning, me and Karter had sex for 3 hours straight. If I didn't know nothing about Karter, I knew everything about him sexually. From 3:15am to roughly about 6:30am we made what felt like love...LUST.

The moment we finished, Karter went to sleep, and I rolled over on my back. Tears flowed silently from my eyes as I prayed.

"God forgive me for what I've just done. Forgive me for sleeping with a man, who cares nothing for me, my son or my body. Father God, from this day forward, I promise that I would never give my body to another man other than my husband. Please grant me more of your Grace to gain self-control and take your way out of temptation. Father God, whenever my hormones arise, and the urge grows strong within my flesh, strengthen me to place my flesh under subjection. Father God, your word says; *Temptation comes from our own desires, which entice us and drags us away. - James 1:14 NLT*

This I know is true because lately…for a long time now, I've been itching, crying and always thinking about it. Father God, When I'm tempted I just want to remain focused on you. I desire take your way out of temptation. Father, your word says; *Keep watch and pray, so that you will not give in to temptation. For the spirit is willing but the body is weak.* - *Mark 14:38 NLT*

So please help me to store your word deep within my heart. When I am tempted, I desire stand on your Word. I desire to submit my whole body to you. Please Father! I deserve better then to be treated or even treat myself like a piece of meat! I am so disgusted with myself. Please help me! I'm just tired of everything and I feel trapped! I just want to be free! Please!" I prayed.

I got up and looked at Karter.

"You make me sick to my stomach" I whispered.

To be honest, that's how I felt about myself.

Around noon, me and Karter both woke up. He left, and I got in the shower. Getting out the shower, I checked my phone to see if I had any missed calls. 3 missed calls from Prophetess Blind and 1 message on Facebook from Diana.

"Oh Jesus, Prophetess Blind knows that I just had sex with Karter. I'm not gone hear the last of this. I wonder what

Diana want. Maybe she found more apartments and jobs for me, let's see" I said to myself.

I opened Diana message;

"I am just going to say this. I will leave you with the decision-making. You need to listen to sound doctrine. The enemy is on your neck. He's trying to hold you back from doing the Will of God. You need to listen to sound doctrine. Your leaders are here to do nothing more than to help you. If you continue to be disobedient you will suffer the consequences. God will curse you! Read *Deuteronomy 28*. This is a message from God himself that he told me to give you" she wrote.

"Wow! Where did this come from and what is she talking about? I wonder do Prophetess Blind complains about me the way she does everybody else. If she does, I really believe she does it with Diana" I thought to myself.

I really didn't know what to say back. It was something about Diana that didn't sit well with me. I didn't trust her. I know I didn't know her to not trust her, but I just didn't. Prophetess Blind complained about her a lot but that wasn't the reason why I didn't trust her. It was something else. I didn't want to not respond, so I messaged her back.

"Ok" I replied.

It's amazing how I haven't heard from Diana for almost 2months now, regarding apartments and jobs. However, the minute I tell Prophetess Blind I don't want to move in with her, here comes Diana giving me a speech about listening to sound doctrine. Things were slowly beginning to make sense. I felt that I had more than enough evidence. However, I wasn't strong enough to say anything just yet.

Headed out to pick up my sister and babies from Renee house, Faith called me.

"Hey Shamika, I'm free tomorrow morning and I will be by your house. Do you want to meet at the library, so I can get started on your taxes?" she asked.

"Hey Faith, Yes. That would be perfect. I switched shifts today, so I work overnight. I will call you when I get off work in the morning" I said.

"Ok cool" she responded.

The following day, I met Faith at the library. We both talked and laughed about our childhood memories, as she prepared my taxes.

"Shamika! Girl you not gone believe how much you getting back!" she said.

"Faith, you crazy lol how much girl! How much?!" I laughed.

"$8,500.00" she said.

"OMG!" I yelled.

"Yes girl! You're only $400.00 away from $9,000. What you gone do with all this money?" she asked.

"I'm going to use it to move and get settled in North Carolina" I said.

"Dang! All of it though? This a lot of money. Well I hope whatever you do, you enjoy spending your money because you deserve this girl" she said.

"Naw, not all of it. I'm not taking nothing with me. Just me and my boys' clothes. I plan to fly there for the first time. I should have plenty left to get everything we need" I explained.

"Aw ok. Look at you! You got it all under control huh?" she laughed.

"lol yes, I do" I said.

I wish that I could've been excited as much as Faith was. That was a lot of money, more money than I ever had in my life. I wasn't good with money and I knew nothing about saving. I didn't want to get this money and blow it.

"When I get this money, I am going to spend it wisely. Whatever it is, if I don't need it, I'm not buying it. I need to budget in everything I do" I said to myself.

When I made it home, I sat on my couch and glanced through my house. It was so dull and dry. My home didn't feel like a home. I was giving everything away to Prophetess Blind for the clothes drive. I was still giving away things that was in good condition. I haven't heard anything about the clothes drive in months. I'm not sure if she was lying just for me to give her all my stuff or what. While sitting, I realized that I ran out of tissue and paper towels. This was weird because I never ran out of house supplies. I always kept loads of house supplies to last me at least 6 months. I decided to go to Walmart. Pulling up to Walmart looking for a park, Prophetess Blind called me.

"Hey baby girl! You busy?" she said.

"Hey! No, not really. What's going on?" I said.

"(Sigh) I was able to prepare our taxes yesterday. It doesn't look like we're getting much back" she said.

"If you don't mind me asking, how much you getting back?" I asked.

"$5,000 and you said the moving fee was about $3,000. That only leaves us with $2,000. We still have to drive there and buy food. That's not enough, especially not for me and my family. I have a big family" she explained.

"Wow! Well everything will be fine. I am sure God will make a way" I said.

"And then, last night my stove went out. My husband called around to see how much another stove would be. The man said it would be $200 for a used one and $700 for a brand new one. I don't want a used stove, the one I have is used and this is what happens. The devil knows he is busy, anything to distract me from doing the Will of God" she said.

"Wow! I don't know what to say" I said.

"You see, you're not the only one going through over there. It may seem like it but it's not only you. Enough about me, how was your day? Were you able to do your taxes?" she asked.

"My day is going good so far. Yes, my cousin just finished preparing my taxes. She couldn't submit them. She gave me an amount of what I'd be getting back though" I said.

"Really?! How much are you getting back?" she asked.

"$8,500" I responded.

"Wow! That's a lot. What are you going to do with all that money?" she said.

"That's the same thing my cousin asked me. I am going to use it to move and get settled. I can now pay off my rent like I planned for the one apartment that I found. That's the one I really want though" I said.

"Can I ask you something?" she asked.

"Yes" I said.

"What was the real reason behind you not wanting to live with me when we move to North Carolina?" she asked.

"What do you mean? I told you the real reason, I need my own space" I responded.

"Shamika…What's the real reason?" she asked.

"Ok, I'm not sure what you mean by what's the real reason. There are other reasons why I don't want to live with you though" I said.

"Ok, what's that?" she asked.

"Your house is a bit nasty and your kids are messy. They don't seem to know when to give people space and you have a dog. My son wouldn't be able to breathe, and I would lose my mind. It doesn't seem that your family know how to clean correctly and that alone will drive me insane. That's why I said I needed my own space" I explained.

"Wow! Just stab me in the heart! I am not that bad Shamika! Wow!" she said.

"I am not trying to stab anyone in the heart. You asked me. I am just being honest. You right, you're not that bad, I never said you were" I said.

"Ok, baby girl. Go ahead with your day. I will talk to you later" she said.

"Ok" I responded.

After shopping at Walmart, I went home, showered and went to sleep. I dreamed that I was in Prophetess Blind house, standing in her bedroom. I watched her as she laid down, dressed in all black. She was on the phone with Diana and they were talking about me. I couldn't hear all of what they were saying but it wasn't good. I got up by the sound of my phone ringing, it was Prophetess Blind.

"Shamika, are you busy?" she asked.

"No. Is everything alright?" I said.

"Yes, everything is fine. You know that house you emailed me…the big white one?" she said.

"Yes, what about it?" I asked.

"I sent Diana to look at it. She said that address doesn't even exist. She stated that it was nothing but a vacant lot" she said.

"That's impossible! Maybe she went to the wrong address. That house had just been posted. Did she call the landlord?" I said.

"I'm not sure. As far as the moving fee, just forget about it because I can't afford that. I'm over here eating from the microwave and electric cookers due to my stove being out. I just don't have time for anything else. Thank You for your time baby girl. You've done all you could do" she said.

"Listen, don't worry about the moving fee and the stove. I will buy it when I get my taxes. I will be getting a lot more than I expected anyway. Just remain focused on God. I will keep searching for more houses as well. Just stay focused on God" I said.

"Really? OMG! Are you sure?" she asked.

"Yes" I responded.

"Shamika, Thank you so much! My God! My God! Thank You, baby girl!" she said.

I wasn't sure what I had just got myself into. However, anything to not hear her complaining and throwing a tantrum. I always felt like if she wasn't in the face of God, I wouldn't be able to learn about him. I just wanted her to focus on God and nothing else. Back at work, my manager; Marie, pulled me to the side.

"Hey Shamika, one of the girls quit. I had to do some small adjustments to the schedule temporarily. From now on you will work Thursday, Friday and Saturday 6am-2pm as normal. Sundays and Mondays, I need you to work overnights 10pm-6am. You will be off on Tuesdays and Wednesdays. It's just until I find someone who is willing to work the overnight shift. Would you be able to do this temporarily?" she asked.

"Well I don't have a choice, I need my job and I'm unable to work the mid-shift. Yes, I can do it temporarily" I responded.

"Ok. Thank You" she said.

The new year was approaching fast. It was just 3 days away. I had nothing planned, I was off New Year's Eve, but I had to work New Year's Day. On New Year's Eve at around 10pm, I was already in bed when a strange number called me. I stared at the phone wondering who could it be, but I didn't answer. Shortly after, I received a text message;

"Shamika! It's me…Miya! Can you answer the phone please, I have something to say? I really need to get this off my chest" she said.

I sat up in my bed not knowing what to do.

"I can't believe after all this time Miya is reaching out to me" I thought to myself.

Now I spoke to Miya awhile back. However, I needed some space. When I told her she immediately thought I was rejecting her. She started going off on me about how I always turn on her. Even though me and Miya talked from time to time, she didn't trust me. Our friendship wasn't the same anymore. I just couldn't be around someone whose intentions wasn't good for me. She hated me, I knew it and I distanced myself from her. I called Prophetess Blind to tell her about this and get her opinion about this situation.

"Hey, You busy?" I asked.

"No, you ok?" she said.

"I think so…Guess who just called me" I said.

"Hmmmm…Miya?" she guessed.

"Yes! Miya called me!" I said.

"Well what happen? What did she say?" she asked.

"I don't know…I didn't answer. I watched as she called" I said.

"lol girl… Shamika, call her back and see what she has to say" she laughed.

"Ok, but before I call her back. Do you think we will ever be friends again?" I asked.

"No. I don't think that would ever be possible. Miya has a hard time with letting things go. You see she held on to this for 5 years. I just don't think she's going to let go and forgive you anytime soon. Call her back, it doesn't hurt to hear what she has to say" she said.

"Ok" I responded.

I called Miya back.

"Hello, hey Miya. Everything alright? I asked.

"Hey Shamika, yes everything is fine. I know you didn't recognize my number. I never thought I would, but I changed it. Anyway, I was calling you to apologize for everything that happened. Shamika, I feel so lost and drained. It's all because I refuse to forgive and let go of a lot of things. I'm so sorry Shamika. If you ever need me, I will be here for you. If you ever need to talk about whatever, I'm here to listen" she said.

"I accept your apology Miya. If I ever did anything to you that made you feel a certain way, I apologize. Its takes a lot to realize your faults and apologize for them. I am proud of you. This is the first step to breaking free from those chains of unforgiveness. I forgive you and I accept your apology. Thank you for calling" I said.

"Ok, thank you for listening" she said.

Getting off the phone with Miya, I realized how easy it was for me to tell her the first step to forgiving. I haven't even taken that step myself when it came to my mom. I don't think Miya even knew why she was angry with me. It wasn't her fault what happened the day we were drinking. It was me, I was angry and hurt looking for someone to blame.

Miya happened to be there, and I made her my target. I'm not sure if she told her sister what happened or not, I just assumed. I felt afraid, ashamed and threatened every time someone asked me about my mom. I assumed people knew what happened between me and my mom even if they didn't.

It made me angry all over again. I would try to hurt others verbally, emotionally and mentally because that's how my mother did me. Anytime I said or did something to others in a bad way, it cut them deep. It caused them to walk around hurt. I didn't care though, hell, I didn't even care about myself.

Miya taught me something without even knowing it. I wanted to forgive and let go of everything. This had been going on for a long time now. I didn't want to go another year carrying this pain. It seemed like I was only suffering even more. I made up in my mind that I was letting go and moving forward. Whether I knew why my mom hurt me or not. I just wanted to forgive her and move forward in my life.

Chapter Nine

The following Sunday, we were already in the year of 2017. During service, Prophetess Blind was the one doing the preaching.

"Today is going to be a little bit different. I want to talk to you all. God has given me a word for each of you. I want to start off by saying God has been good to me. The enemy has been very busy due to the move getting closer. I was worried about a lot in which I shouldn't have been. Just when I was about to give up, God made a way. I don't have to worry about the moving fee, its paid in full. God has made a way for my family to get a new stove. That was all I had been praying for, especially this move" she explained.

Listening to Prophetess Blind, it hit me when she said God basically paid for everything and made a way for her and her family.

"Is that true? I was the one who willingly said I would pay for everything. Well maybe it was God moving in me to do a good thing. What if, I would've never suggested though? Would she still be saying the same thing, or would she be frustrated? Would she even be up there preaching right now, or would Elder Blind be up there?" I thought to myself.

Prophetess Blind continued speaking.

"Malcom, God has called you to be a Joseph. He has chosen you to go to a land beforehand. You will go and prepare. When you call for your family, they will come. Your family won't have to worry about anything. You have always been the one set apart from the rest of your brothers. Your mother knows it too. When you and your brothers leave that house, there is not a day that goes by that she doesn't pray over you all" she said.

"Yep! That's true! There were days that I got off work early. I would be in the basement and I would hear her praying" said Anna.

"You know something, when you say that "I have always been the one set apart from my brothers" it just dawned on me how I went to different schools from them growing up. My mother dressed me a certain way and there were certain things I just couldn't do. She wasn't strict or anything, she was just careful with me. I always had a unique style and mindset from my brothers. Not that there's any competition or anything like that. I just noticed that I'm different and I like different things" said Malcolm.

Listening to Prophetess Blind and Malcolm talk, I got very emotional. For some reason I started to think about my family. I wasn't very close with anyone apart of my family except my grandma, yet the thought of leaving them made me very sensitive. I held my tears back and pulled myself together.

"I wonder will my family come if I ever called for them" I thought to myself.

I didn't want my story to be Malcolm's story. However, I at least wanted my family to be apart of what God had in store for me. I wanted to share my blessings he had in store for me with them. Prophetess Blind continued;

"Shamika" she said.

Shocked that she called my name, I looked up.

"Yes" I responded.

"Can you come sit up here a little closer to me?" she asked.

"Yes, I responded.

I always sat in the last row to the back of her living room during service. I moved up closer and sat next to Malcolm. It was the second row from where Prophetess Blind stood. She looked at me directly in my eyes and smiled.

"God is going to replace your ashes for beauty. I know your mother has installed a hurtful wound inside of you. I know that it has caused you to put up many walls. Its so easy for you to block out everyone around you, even God himself. Shamika, God loves you and he understands. For every negative word spoken against you, it will not touch you. It will hit the ground. God will restore and heal you. You have to be willing to let go of the past and let him in" she said.

"Ok" I responded.

Hearing Prophetess Blind say these things to me made me feel like I was somebody. If God felt this way about me, I must've meant a lot to him. I must've been worth more than how I seen myself. I must've been loved by him more then I even loved myself. I had no idea what love was or felt like but whatever it was… God was a part of it.

That night at work, I replayed what was said at service continuously in my mind. I thought about my family and my mom. Those tears that I held back during service, fell from my eyes uncontrollably as they deluged my work desk. I normally slept most of my overnight shifts away, but this night was different. I stayed up my whole shift.

"I wonder what God have in store for me. I wonder what's God's Will for me. I know his Will for this church is for us to move to North Carolina. I feel like this is all wrong. I feel like there is something different he desires for me to do. Am I wrong for feeling this way? I just need to stop with all this overthinking. It just feels so awkward though" I said to myself.

Working overnights, I was completely alone in the whole building. I wasn't crazy or anything like that, I just really enjoyed thinking out loud. Sitting at my work desk I prayed.

"Father God, I know you probably heard me talking about it just now but I'm curious to know one thing. This will be weird because out of all the things I asked, I'm not sure if I asked you this before. Father, what is your Will for me? What is it that you desire for me to do as an individual? I know for the church that I am a part of, your Will is for us all to move to North Carolina…. or is it? I'm sorry if I'm asking to many questions or for even questioning you period. To be honest, I just wish I knew you better. Forgive me for asking this but do I really need Prophetess Blind to get to you? Is it wrong to just come straight to you on my own? Father, Help me please! Since I've been a part of this ministry things have gotten worse. I don't know but I thought it was supposed to be different. I thought I was supposed to be learning more about you and drawing closer to you. I thought healing and deliverance was supposed to be taking place. Father, every time I turn around, I don't have any money to pay my bills. I'm always being told what is and what's not your Will. I can't talk to anybody, not even my family. I blocked my mother not really wanting to. She tried to reconciliate, but I threw out her gift. Prophetess

Blind stated that it would harm me. Is that true? I just feel like something is weighing me down. Is this how its suppose to feel while doing your Will? Father God, All I want is you. Whatever it is that you desire for me to do, can you please grant me more of your Grace to be faithful in doing it? Father, please show me, speak to me and share with me your thoughts regarding everything I am bringing forth to you" I prayed.

Nevertheless, listen to my prayer and my plea, O Lord my God. Hear the cry and the prayer that your servant is making to you today. -1 Kings 8:28 NLT

After work, I picked up my babies, went home and went to sleep.

"Ma! Can we come in your room and sleep with you?" asked David.

Restlessly, I hopped up by the sound of his voice, but I couldn't see anything.

"Yes, you and Keith come in here with me" I responded.

"Ma! Are you ok?" he asked.

"Yes. I'm just really tired" I replied.

I went back to sleep. Although I slept well when I woke up by the sound of my alarm, my body was hot.

"David! Keith! Get up! We have to go!" I yelled.

"God! I'm burning up! And I'm thirsty!" I yelled as I rubbed my neck and chest.

I sat up in my bed… as I got up, I stumbled.

"Ma! Are you ok!?" yelled David.

"I feel so weak and dizzy. I don't think I will be able to make it to work tonight. Go get me a bottled water. I'm so thirsty and hot. Is y'all hot or is it just me?" I asked.

"No, we not hot. I think it's just you, Ma" he said.

"Ok" I responded.

"Ma, when we came in your room earlier today. You hopped up and asked me who was I…then you laid back down and went to sleep. You scared me, and Keith started crying. That's why I kept asking you, are you ok?" David explained.

"I did? I don't remember me doing that. I remember me telling you that y'all can come in here with me and that's it. I'm sorry, David. I didn't mean to scare you or Keith. I don't know what's going on with me" I responded.

"Me neither, but it's alright" he said.

Keith hopped on me and wrapped his little arms around me.

"Mommy, give me kiss" he said.

"Muah! Muah! Muah!" I kissed him.

Keith was 2 years old. He was about to be 3 in 2weeks. I loved my baby so much. Both of my boys made me feel secured. With everything I was dealing with, having them both, kept me going.

That night, I texted my manager.

"Marie, I'm sorry but I will no longer be coming to work anymore"

There is no good reason as to why I quit my job. I was going through mentally, emotionally and spiritually. I just needed a break from everything and everybody.

"Now, maybe I could rest" I thought to myself.

That night I dreamed of me standing on top of a big rock centered in the river. The water was so fresh and clean as it silently flowed pass my feet. I looked around to get a clear glance at where I was at. From afar, I seen a white house with huge white pillars surrounding it.

Not really knowing how I got out of the river, I kept my eyes on this house, as I ran towards it. The faster I ran, the closer the house seemed. When I stopped the further the house was away. I decided to stop running and walk.

Still keeping my eyes on the house, I noticed I was beginning to walk through tall green grass. Slightly, as I took my eyes off the house, I looked to the right side of me and there flowed the river. Looking up, placing my eyes back on the house, I realized that I was getting closer.

I woke up by the sound of my phone ringing uncontrollably. Looking at my clock, it was only 6:30am. Feeling around in my bed for my phone,

"Who is this calling me?" I said to myself.

It was Prophetess Blind.

"Hello" I said.

"Hey baby girl, how was work?" she asked.

There was a moment of silence. Hearing her ask me this question made me realize I made a crazy decision by quitting my job.

"Hello! Shamika! You there?" she asked.

"Yes, I'm here" I responded.

"Is everything alright?" she asked.

"No, it's not. Something came over me last night and I quit my job" I explained.

"What! Shamika! Nooooo!" she yelled.

"I know...but I got up dizzy and I could barely walk. I was hot, and I don't know what was wrong. I'm sorry" I cried.

"Shamika! Why would you quit your job? Whatever you were feeling is a part of life. We all go through things, that doesn't mean just stop and give up" she said.

"I know, but you don't understand. I couldn't move and I'm just tired of all of this. I just want to stay home away from everyone and just rest" I said.

"Shamika, how are you going to live? You have kids to provide for. You have bills, what are you going to do?" she asked.

"I will be fine. Everything will be alright. I know it will. I just need to rest, that's all" I said.

"Alright Shamika! Go ahead and get you some rest. I will talk to you later" she said sarcastically.

Prophetess Blind seemed more upset than me and I was the one who was now jobless. She was more concerned about how I was going to pay and provide then how I was feeling. Maybe I should've thought this out before making a final decision. All I wanted was to rest and have some sort of peace. I didn't care about anything else.

The following week, I slept my days away. I only got up when it was time to drop off and pick up my babies from school. I still attended service on Sundays, but something still felt awkward. Something within my spirit just didn't feel right. I still didn't know what it could've been.

Sitting in service, I listened as Elder Blind preached.

"The bible says a doubled minded man is unstable…in what? all his ways, right? We cannot make decisions in life without first going before God. It's about his Will and what he wants us to do, not what we want. We need to talk with our leaders always before we make a choice. If we refuse, we'll continuously find ourselves suffering the consequences" he said.

I sat up straight through the whole service and gave him direct eye contact as he preached.

"Wow! I guess todays Word is for me. Last week, it was for Diana and the week before that, it was for Malcolm and Anna. I just love how they manipulate the Word of God to get what they want" I thought to myself.

After service, I went straight home and went to sleep. I woke up at 2am, used the bathroom and checked my phone. I had 2 missed calls from Prophetess Blind and a message on Facebook. I decided to check my message first. I really didn't want to be bothered with Prophetess Blind. I figured I would just call her back in a couple of hours. My Facebook message was from Diana.

"Hey, someone apart of the ministry needs help with house supplies no later than this Sunday. If you can please provide any tissue, paper towels, soap and cleaning products. Leave everything at Prophetess Blind house. Thank You" she said.

Now, I didn't respond back to the message, instead I wondered who was it that needed help. It was only Me, Malcom, Anna, Terry, Diana and Tia that was a part of the ministry. Me, Anna, Malcolm and Prophetess Blind lived in Chicago. Tia moved from Florida to Italy. Diana and Terry lived in North Carolina. I had just purchased house supplies, so it wasn't me. Malcom and Anna lived with Malcom's family. He had a big family, so I'm sure if they ran out of anything, everyone worked together to provide. It wasn't Tia or Diana and Terry, they stayed out of town

My first mind told me that it was Prophetess Blind. Instead of waiting to call her back, I immediately called to see was everything alright.

"Hey, Is everything alright? I asked.

"Hey Shamika, yes everything is fine. Why do you ask that?" she said.

"Diana sent me a message. It stated that someone apart of the ministry needs help with house supplies. It's not too many of us apart of the ministry, so I figured it was you, is it you?" I said.

"Well you've guessed right, it's me. Things got a little rough and my husband was unable to buy house supplies this time around. I decided to ask for help" she explained.

"Aw ok, why didn't you just ask me? I was out shopping for house supplies not too long ago" I said.

"You don't have a job anymore, so it wouldn't do me any good asking you" she said.

"What does me not having a job have to do with me helping you? I could've made a way to get you what you needed" I said.

"Well I called but you didn't answer, so I decided to call Diana instead. Besides, I don't want to be a burden" she said nonchalantly.

"Ok. Did you let Diana know what you needed specifically because you know how you can get when it's not what you want?" I asked.

"What's that supposed to mean!? And no, I didn't tell her about anything specifically. I will be grateful for whatever everyone gives" she said.

"I just know how you are. I know how you like certain things to be, that's why I asked but ok. Let me know if you need anything extra" I said.

"Ok. This week counseling session will be cancelled. It will resume next Thursday" she said.

"Ok" I responded.

"I can't believe she said that to me. I guess now since I'm not working, I'm not good for anything" I thought to myself.

That morning when I went back to sleep, I dreamed of something different this time. I had a dream that I was in the car with Elder and Prophetess Blind. They were trying to take me to get my babies. Elder Blind was driving but

Prophetess Blind was directing the way he should go. They kept arguing because every turn she told him to make, led us into traffic. We were sitting in heavy traffic and the light refused to turn green.

Looking at the time, I realized that I was running late. It dawned on me that even if I wanted to, I couldn't sit in traffic with them any longer. While listening to them argue, I kept looking at the traffic and the time. I knew I wasn't going to make it with them, so I got out the car and caught the train. When I arrived at my babies' school, I stood in line. The security guard approached me.

"Why are you late?" he asked.

"I'm so sorry. My pastor was trying to give me a ride, but he just kept making the wrong turn" I explained.

"Are you aware that there is a late fee?" he asked.

"Yes I am. Can you please spare me some time? I don't have it today, but I promise I will pay it" I said.

"You know what, don't worry about it. I will let you pass this time" he said while smiling.

I grabbed my babies and left. I woke up later that afternoon. Laying in my bed I decided to have a talk with God.

"Jesus, are you saying that Elder and Prophetess Blind are not equipped to lead? Maybe it's just me. Maybe I'm overthinking when it comes to these dreams that I'm having. Father, I'm not sure why but something still feels awkward. I've been getting plenty of rest, yet I still feel entangled. Father, if something isn't right move in me and allow me to have your discernment" I prayed.

The following week, I started reading my bible more. Prophetess Blind would normally email out a newsletter with assigned readings from the bible. I noticed most of the readings where from the old testament regarding the mosaic law. At times she would switch it up and add readings from the book of Psalms, Proverb, Matthew and Romans.

I wanted to dig deeper in the word of God, so I downloaded the You Version app. I updated my old profile and I started to search for different bible plans. I wanted to have a dose of God's word each day. I was home now with nothing else to do. I figured why not get to know who God is during this down time.

One morning after dropping my babies off to school, I was headed to do laundry. I was starting to feel much better. I hadn't spoken to Prophetess Blind since last week. For some reason, it's like when I didn't speak to her, I felt good. When I did talk to her, I felt weighed down all over again. While doing laundry, she called me.

"Hey baby girl, have you been getting some rest lately?" she asked.

"Yes, actually I have. How is everything going with you?" I responded.

"You don't even want to know. I have been very irritated lately. I just don't understand why people choose to do the church the way that they do" she said.

"What do you mean by that? Is everything alright?" I asked.

"Well remember last week when Diana sent out that message regarding me needing help. Malcolm and Anna decided to go to the dollar store. They brought all this cheap stuff that I don't even use. This is not enough for me and my family. Matter fact let me send you a picture of it" she said.

"Wow! That's why I asked you were you specific with what you needed. You stated that you would be grateful with whatever you receive" I said.

Yes, I know. I didn't think they would go to the dollar store though. I mean everything they brought came from the dollar store even the washing detergent. Why do people do the church like this?" she said.

"Pastor, listen…I'm sure if you were specific with what items that you preferred, Malcom and Anna would've gotten you just that. Since you weren't, they just went out and grabbed you whatever. They probably didn't even know it was for you. If I'm not mistaken, Diana never mentioned who, she just stated someone apart of the ministry needs help" I explained.

"Yea, but what difference does it make? When Diana said the keyword "Ministry" they should have thought of the church regardless of who it was for. They should have shopped as if it was for them" she said.

"Well maybe that's how they shop for themselves, you never know. Maybe the dollar store is where they go for supplies, everyone is different" I said.

"Shamika, please just stop! Really! Just look at the clothes, shoes and things that Anna buy. Does that look like it came from the dollar store? …no, it doesn't. She spends good money when it comes to her and so does Malcolm" she said sarcastically.

"Ok, well is there anything I can get you that you don't have?" I asked while trying to end the conversation.

"Lol, yes baby girl and that would be everything" she laughed.

"Can you be specific?" I asked.

"I need paper towels…Bounty paper towels, to be exact. Lysol disinfected spray, armor hammer carpet cleaner and 4 containers of Ajax. If you are led by God to buy anything else, please do so" she said.

"Ok, I get my last check this Friday. Hopefully I will be able to get everything you need and more" I said.

"Ok, Thank You baby girl. Go ahead with your day. I love you" she said.

"Ok" I responded.

The following morning before everyone got off the prayer line, Prophetess Blind made an announcement.

"God has called a fast and it will start next Monday. This fast won't be like last one. He has decided to loosen up on us. We can eat meat only if its fish. We can also use our normal seasonings. The first week will be fish and vegetables only. I will give you all further instructions regarding the week after very soon. Alright you all, have a blessed day. We will talk soon" she said.

I had never been excited about fasting but for some reason this time, I was. The moment I received my link, I gave

Prophetess Blind her ten percent. That left me with enough for everything I needed… at least that's what I thought. I did most of my grocery shopping at Jewel Osco. After purchasing fish and vegetables, I only had $50.38 left. I had just received my link and it was basically gone. I still had to purchase my babies' food as well because they weren't fasting. I spent the last of my link grabbing my babies some of their favorite food items.

"If I run out of food I will just use my last check to purchase more food" I thought to myself.

During prayer, Prophetess Blind spoke more about the fast.

"God is going to show us all ourselves. He will also speak regarding this move to North Carolina. Be mindful and listen out for him because he will speak" she said.

I was curious to see what God had to say regarding me and this move. To be honest, I didn't feel right about moving. I felt like this was something Prophetess Blind came up with. I felt like she was trying to manipulate everyone into believing it was God so that we would not resist. Although, I felt this way, I didn't feel that I had enough evidence to say something about it. I was anxious for God to show me myself. I desired more of him and all I wanted was a pure heart. All I wanted was to know what love was and be able to love myself. All I wanted was to be at peace and filled with joy. I didn't care about anything else. I just wanted to forgive and be forgiven.

I wanted my motives to be pure in everything that I did. I didn't want to be angry and constantly hold on to my past. I desired for all my inside wounds to be healed. All I wanted was to be delivered and set free. I knew deep down inside that no one can fill these many voids in me but God. This fast was my opportunity to get all up in his face and spend all my time with him.

Before I knew It, Friday was here. I was up early anxious to check my account. My check was only $442.98. It dawned on me that I quit my job without working a full 2 weeks. I was behind in my rent and my lights. My phone bill was due as well. I know I told Prophetess Blind I would get what she needed when I got my last check. However, my check balance was unexpected. I sat up that morning trying to figure out how was I going to get her stuff and pay my bills. While trying to think things over, Prophetess Blind called me.

"Good morning baby girl, did I wake you?" she said.

"No. I just got up. Is everything alright?" I responded.

"No, it's not. The alternator went out in our van and my husband had to miss work. He's out there now trying to figure out what's going on" she explained.

"Oh wow! I'm sorry to hear that. Why did he miss work? He could've took the bus" I said.

"I know but he got up in enough time expecting to drive and he don't have bus fare. He had just put the last of our money in the van for gas" she said.

"Oh wow!" I responded.

"Did you pay your tithes this morning? I didn't receive anything from you" she said.

"No, not yet. My check wasn't what it would normally be. I quit without working 2 full weeks. I am trying to figure out if I would have enough to pay my tithes and bills altogether" I explained.

"Listen, you have to pay your tithes first no matter what! Let God handle the rest. Don't worry about anything" she said.

"Would God be angry with me if I missed this one time from paying my tithes? I just really don't have it. I'm already behind in my bills" I said.

"Shamika, you can't pick and choose when you will and will not pay your tithes. I know you may not have much, but you must give God his ten percent no matter what. He will make a way for you to pay your bills. Are you still buying the house supplies?" she said.

There was a moment of silence.

Listening to Prophetess Blind, this conversation reminded me of the conversation we had regarding her Christmas layaway. Although she acted like she cared, she really didn't care at all. She would always say God would make a way. If that's the case, why did she call on me every time something went wrong with her financially. Knowing the type of heart I have; she knew all she had to do was sound sentimental. Eventually I would offer to help without her fully coming out to ask. I believed that if anything was to ever go wrong, she would play the victim. She would make it like she never asked for anything and I was always the one offering. I was starting to realize that although she came off loving and caring… she was like a wolf dressed in sheep clothing slowly devouring me. I knew better but I kept on as if I didn't.

Beware of false prophets who come disguised as harmless sheep but are really vicious wolves. -Matthew 7:15 NLT

"Can I call you right back? I just need to look over this to see if I will have enough" I said.

"Shamika, when you take care of your leaders, God will provide for you. You have nothing to worry about. If you have anything left over, can you help towards this alternator or maybe even bus fare so that my husband can get to work?" she asked.

"I will call you back and let you know, how much is the alternator?" I said.

"$260.00" she said.

"Ok. I will call you back" I said.

"Ok baby girl, I love you" she said.

"Ok" I responded.

Getting off the phone, I immediately wrote everything down that I had to pay.

Out of $442.98
-tithes $44.29
-alternator $260.00
-phone bill $60.00
-light bill $$1265.00 (just put $60 on it)
-rent (don't worry about)

After doing the math I was only left with $18.69 for a whole month, at least until I received my taxes. I didn't know how I was going to make it, but I didn't worry about it. I just didn't want my pastor to have to worry about anything. Immediately, I called Prophetess Blind back.

"Hey Pastor, I will give you the money for your alternator. I will drop off the money once I take my boys to school. So maybe around 9:30/10c'clock" I said.

"Ok, thank you. What about the house supplies?" she asked.

"OMG! I forgot all about that! Ok, wait maybe I can call my auntie Vicky. Anytime I ask her for anything, she gives it to me. I will ask her for a couple of dollars to get your house supplies" I said.

"Oh ok. I will see you soon" she said.

It's amazing how she didn't want me to talk to my family. However, it seemed as though when it was beneficial for her, it was alright. After getting off the phone I texted Vicky.

"Hey Vicky, I hope all is well. I need your help. I paid all my bills and I was only left with $18.69. I still have to buy house supplies though, is there any way that you could loan me $75.00 until the next time I get paid" I said.

Vicky responded immediately.

"Sure thing, I will drop off the money tonight before I go to work" she said.

"Ok, thanks" I responded.

After dropping my boys off to school, I stopped at the bank. I, then headed to Prophetess Blind house. When I arrived, Elder Blind let me in. I walked into Prophetess Blind bedroom and there she was laying in her bed. I handed the money to her, however she insisted that I give it to Elder Blind. He counted the money and looked at me.

"Are you sure you have this money to give?" he asked.

"Yes, I responded.

"Ok, well thank you. We appreciate you" he said.

"No problem" I said.

"Do you have somewhere that you need to be? I was going to ask can you take me to pick up the alternator" he said.

"No, I don't have anything to do. You can go ahead and use my car. I will wait until you comeback" I said while handing him my car keys.

"Ok, I shouldn't be gone long. I will be back in about an hour maybe sooner than that" he said.

"Ok, take your time" I responded.

I sat down on a stool next to her bed and watched the tv show "Chicago Fire" with her.

"This is one of my favorite shows. This and Chicago Meds. I have them all recorded, I love these shows" she said.

"Really, what are they about" I asked.

"Just basically different series of what goes on in Chicago behind closed doors with doctor, lawyers and firefighters" she explained.

"Aww ok" I responded.

"Quick question: So, the money that you gave for the alternator was that included with your tithes or is that considered an offering" she said.

"It's altogether, so yea… you can say it's an offering" I responded.

"Aw ok because see I don't want you to get the two mixed up. I'm just making sure" she said.

"Ok" I said.

"So, tell me, what were yours thought last Sunday when I gave you all an individual word from God" she asked.

"I was surprised but I felt a little better, I guess. I got a bit emotional though when you started talking about mothers and family" I said.

"I know. I knew something was wrong just by the look on your face" she said.

"I just don't understand any of this. I never blocked my mother regardless of what she has done. It's bothering me and I'm not at peace with it" I said.

"Shamika…Listen, it's all for your good. Your mother spirit is not right towards you. I just don't want you to get hurt any more than you already are. You can unblock her once we move and get settled. Shamika…Listen, this is your real family. We are your family in Christ and that's all that matters" she said.

"Yea but what about my mom? What about my grandma? Can I at least bring my grandma? If I left the rest of my family it wouldn't bother me. If I have my grandma with me I will feel much better" I explained.

"Sure, you can bring your grandma, but I doubt if she come. You can't force her, Shamika. Listen, baby girl, I am your mother. Everyone apart of this ministry is your real family. You cannot worry about your family. Look at how they try to stop you from doing the Will of God. Do you really think they care about you or your relationship with God?" she said.

"I'm not sure what to think anymore. I am just tired of feeling this way" I said.

"Well I am glad you feel the way that you do. God is going to show you all you need to know. He will comfort you like never before during this fast" she said.

"Ok, aw yeah. My auntie is going to drop off the money tonight. I will bring you your house supplies tomorrow morning around this time" I said.

"Ok… do you at least feel a little bit better now that we've talked?" she asked.

"Yes" I lied.

Soon after we finished talking Elder Blind walked in and gave me my car keys. I said my goodbyes and headed home. Riding home, our whole conversation replayed in my mind.

"I can't believe she said she is my mother and the people in this ministry is my real family. What does she mean my mother spirit is not right towards me? Once upon a time, her mother spirit wasn't right towards her, but did she block her out of her life? No, she didn't. I remember her telling me that she didn't let anyone, or anything come between her and her mother. Why should I? Although I don't understand why my mother do me the way she does, I still love her dearly. That's still my mom and no one could ever replace her" I said to myself.

I couldn't believe Prophetess Blind had the audacity to think that the conversation we had helped me feel better. There was not a doubt in my mind that kept me from thinking something suspicious was going on. The next day, I went to Target and brought her house supplies. I dropped everything off to her and headed back home. Later that day, she called me just to say thank you and that service was cancelled. I didn't ask why, to be honest I was glad. I was able to stay in and get in the face of God concerning a lot of things.

Sunday went by quick and before I knew it...it was Monday, the first day of the fast. Prophetess Blind emailed everyone assigned readings, but I was tired of reading about the mosaic law. I wanted to dig deeper in the Word of God. I decided to read about Jesus and his disciples.

The first 4 days of the fast I ate baked tilapia and vegetables. I prayed and mediated on the Word of God day and night. However, the dreams that I was having were only regarding me. I figured God was showing me myself which was perfect. I yearned to know who I was. He had not spoken to me regarding the move.

Thursday evening arrived, and I was all out of food for the fast. My babies still had enough food to last about another day or two. I had no idea where I was going to get food from because I didn't have a dime. I was all out of link. I couldn't ask my neighbor and I couldn't call anyone in my family. That night Prophetess Blind called me for counseling.

"Hey baby girl, are you ready?" she said.

"Yes, I'm ready" I responded.

"Ok, before we get started, I have a question for you. Have your mother or anyone ever express to you, how much they love you? Have anyone ever said the words "I Love You" to you at all?" she asked.

"No" I responded.

"Ok. I was just wondering because I notice when I say I Love You, you never say it back" she said.

"Yes, I know. It sounds good to hear. I really wish I knew how to say it back. I just can't find it in me to say something that I don't mean. I don't even know what Love is" I said.

"Wow! Well I understand baby girl. I just want you to know that I truly genuinely love you from the bottom of my heart. Whether you love me or not, that will never change" she said.

"Ok" I responded.

"So, tell me, what are your thoughts about me being your mother and this ministry being your family in Christ?" she asked.

"I really wasn't sure what to think. I still get emotional when I think about leaving my family though" I said.

"I understand. I feel the same way when I think about leaving my mother. My sisters... I don't too much care about. I know how you feel but just think about what's more important" she said.

"Yes, you're right" I said.

"Well, is there anything that you would like to talk about?" she asked.

"No, not really" I responded.

"Ok, well we will resume next Thursday at the same time. I will talk to you soon... oh wait! Are you getting on the prayer line tonight?" she asked.

"Yes" I said.

"Ok" she said.

That night on the prayer line, Diana led us in prayer.

"We are the praying warriors! Yes! We are the praying warriors! Although we may be going through, we are to pray for one another. God is calling us to pray for one another, no matter what. We shouldn't be bad mouthing anyone, instead we should be praying. We should be asking God to heal, deliver, and lead those who are lost. Thank You Jesus! Hallelujah! Praise God! Father, show us how to pray always. Thank You Jesus! Amen. Alright now, you all be blessed. Good night" she said.

The following morning, I dropped my babies off to school and came back home. I didn't have anything to eat so I drunk water instead. I mediated on God's Word and prayed for about 2 hours straight. While I was reading the Word of God, I stopped and thought about something.

"Wait a minute, if I pay for Prophetess Blind moving expenses and buy her a new stove…am I going to be left with anything?" I thought to myself.

I'm not sure where this thought came from, but it made a lot of sense. I grabbed my notebook and decided to do the math.

Refund amount: $8,500.00

Prophetess Blind Moving expenses: $3,058.00
Prophetess Blind New Stove: $700.00
6-months' rent in North Carolina: $4,188.00

Total Amount leftover: $554.00

"Ok wait a minute $554.00 is not enough for me and my babies to get settled In North Carolina. I still have to pay for our flight. Not to mention, we still need beds, furniture, clothes and food once we arrive there. I was looking into buying a car, getting my ID and driver's licenses. That's not enough to do anything. I'm going to have to talk to Prophetess Blind about this" I said to myself.

After going over everything once more, just to confirm it. I decided to give Prophetess Blind a call.

"Hey, are you busy? I need to talk to you about something" I said.

"Well I was just about to get ready and do someone's hair. I have about 20minutes before I start, I'm not busy. Is everything alright?" she said.

"Not really. I was sitting here going over everything that I would be paying with my taxes. I realize that after paying for your moving expenses, stove and my rent in North Carolina...I will only be left with $554.00. That's not enough for me and babies to survive. There were other bills that I wanted to pay off here in Chicago before I left. I won't be able to do any of that with this amount" I explained.

"Well baby girl, this is the time where you need to get before the Lord and ask him to intervene. With all the bible study session that I've taught I would expect you to already know this. You need to get before God and explain to him that you've been a good steward. You've done nothing but good and you need him to intervene on your behalf…Ok, I will talk to you later. I have to start on this hair" she said.

Getting off the phone, I sat on my living room couch. I was disarrayed by the conversation that had just taken place. I was stunned, and no one could stop me from thinking of how selfish she is. If I gave her the response she just gave me, all hell would've broke loose. I never expected anything in return for anything that I did. However, when it was anything regarding me or how I felt, no one seemed to care. All my life I felt used and abandoned. My mother used me as her target. Karter used me for sex and now Prophetess Blind is using me to get to where she is trying to go. None of this had nothing to do with God.

"I'm done! The only one that I will call on, run to and let use me from this day forward is God" I said to myself.

Heading out to get my babies from school, I grabbed the last water from my refrigerator. I didn't have any food at all, not even can goods. I knew when my boys got home they would be hungry and thirsty. As bad as I wanted to, I couldn't call my mom. I knew that if I called her, she would've came and filled my house up with food. I just didn't have time for her negative remarks. The first thing I felt that she would ask me is why didn't I ask the church that I devoted to for help. If she did ask me that, she had every right to.

"Wait a minute…why am I so hesitant to ask this ministry for help?" I thought to myself.

That night at 9:30pm, I decided to give up my pride and ask Prophetess Blind for help. I decided to text her instead of calling.

"Hey Pastor, I'm not going to be able to continue on with this fast. I ran completely out of food. If you can please go to Aldi and grab me a loaf of bread, a gallon of milk, a bag of potato chips and a pack of lunchmeat. I get these items all the time, it shouldn't cost you no more than $10" I texted.

After sending the text message, Prophetess Blind didn't text me back until a whole hour later.

"Hey Shamika, Yes. That's fine I will go tomorrow morning and get you the food" she replied.

I told David to try and get some sleep on an empty stomach. I explained to him that tomorrow we will have some food. Keith didn't understand but he eventually cried himself to sleep.

"Ma, can you please just call grandma? Please? I'm hungry and thirsty" cried David.

"David, I can't call her" I said.

"Why not? Ma, if you call she will come right now. I know she will...Please I'm hungry" he cried.

"Go in there and go to sleep before you wake Keith up. The pastor said she will bring us the food that I asked for tomorrow morning" I said.

"Ok" he said.

I listened as my babies got up and went back to sleep repeatedly through the night with a cry of hunger. At 3am the following morning, I received a texted from Prophetess Blind.

"Hey Shamika, an unexpected bill came up that I really have to pay. I'm sorry but I'm not going to be able to get you the food. If you want, I can bring you a bag of beans and a box of cornbread from my kitchen" she texted.

"That's alright. Thank you" I responded.

Tears stormed from my eyes as I read over the text. My feelings were hurt. I couldn't believe she said an unexpected bill came up. It may have been true, but I didn't believe that. I'm not sure what was the real reason behind this but something deep within me did not believe that. The fact that she stated an unexpected bill came up hurt me even more. I was behind tremendously with all my bills and my car was slowly falling apart. There was not one time she called me, and I did not help. Even if I couldn't help, I was borrowing money that I couldn't pay back. I made sure she had specifically what she needed.

"Jesus, please just tell me when did this unexpected bill come about? Did she not know this yesterday or the day before? I'm sure if she did, I would've been the first to know about it. Why would she wait until 3 in the morning to tell me about this? Father, I am so angry and hurt. Everything I ever did or gave was to get more of you in return. I never asked for anything but the one time I do, this is what happens. Father, me and my babies are hungry! Please send us some food! Please!" I cried.

A couple of hours later, I woke up by the sound of both my babies crying.

"Mommy, can I have some cereal?" asked Keith.

"Ok, one second" I said.

I couldn't tell my baby there is nothing to eat or drink. He was just a baby, he didn't understand. I had to figure something out quick, but I didn't know where to start. I couldn't call my family out the blue and ask for food. I hadn't spoken to them since November, and that didn't end so well. I was afraid of the negative feedback that I would get from them. I just couldn't handle any extra pressure than what I was already dealing with.

"Ma, did the pastor say what time she would be here with the food? I'm hungry" said David.

"Yes. She will be here in about an hour" I lied.

I just couldn't tell my baby what she did, at least not right now. I was under too much pressure and now wasn't the time to talk about anything. I would've found myself getting angry and I didn't want to be angry anymore.

Around noon, Prophetess Blind sent a group message on Facebook to everyone apart of the ministry.

"Good afternoon Everyone, I have something to say for all of you who have been obedient during this fast. God

is going to bless you. I am proud of you all and I encourage
you to continue on being obedient unto the lord" she said.

"Amen" replied Anna.
"Amen" replied Diana.

Now reading over what Prophetess Blind said. I felt like
she was saying that God wasn't going to bless anyone who
wasn't going through with the fast. I felt like she was
making it seem like I was considered disobedient unto the
Lord. Prophetess Blind knew how much I loved the Lord
and how all I wanted was more of him. I could've been
wrong with the way I was thinking but I felt threatened.
This time I didn't hold back, I defended myself because I
knew deep down inside...I had been her target for a long
time now.

"I believe that God will still bless and speak to
those who are unable to proceed with the fast. I say this
because recently I ran out of food. I am now unable to go
on with the fast, but God is still speaking to me and
showing me myself. I know he understands and I know he
will continue to bless me" I replied.

Shortly after I replied to Prophetess Blind message, Diana
messaged me outside of the group message.

"Do you know that you just said the total opposite of what pastor said? Have you lost your mind? You can't do that. You cannot speak against what she says" she said.

"I am not trying to speak against anyone. I am speaking based off what I know. I have been without food for the fast for 2 days now. God is still speaking to me and showing me things. Therefore, I responded the way I did" I explained.

"What do you mean you've been without food for 2 days? Why haven't you said anything to anyone?" she asked.
"I told the pastor. She said she would get me the food then she texted me at 3am this morning stating that an unexpected bill came up. So, as of now I still have no food and my babies are hungry" I said.

"Shamika, give me one second. I am going to call you so that we can talk about this" she said.

When Diana called me, we weren't on the phone long before her house phone rung. Now before she put me on hold, she listened to everything I was saying. When she arrived back on the phone, she had a very nasty attitude. I knew right then and there she had just spoken to Prophetess Blind on the house phone.

"Listen Shamika, nobody told you to quit your job. Do you realize you brought this upon yourself? I don't have any money. I'm sure Prophetess Blind wouldn't mind helping you, but a bill came up" she said.

"Isn't that a coincidence though? I ask for food...she says yes but when 3am arrives she realizes she have an unpaid bill? I'm sorry but I don't believe that" I said.

"Wait a minute now! You need to slow your role! First off, ain't nothing a coincidence, if she said she have a bill, then that's what it is. Things like this happen all the time because it happens to me. Sometimes it's so much going on that I forget. Shamika, from what I hear you're asking for food that has nothing to do with the fast. Chips and sandwich meat...cum on now, really?!" she said sarcastically.

"I am unable to continue with the fast. I ran out of food completely. I asked for a couple of items that will at least feed my babies" I said.

"You're unable to continue with the fast or you don't want to do the fast. Which one is it?" she asked.

"What are you talking about? I'm unable to continue on with the fast" I responded.

Before Diana responded her house phone rang again. It could've been anybody calling but based off my intuition…it was Prophetess Blind. Diana placed me on hold again for about 5 minutes. When she got back on the phone, she immediately shut our whole conversation down quick.

"Listen, you need to continue on being obedient to your leaders. It's not our fault that you decided to quit your job. Like I said, I don't have any money right now. Send me a list of the food that you need, and I will figure something out. I will message you later today letting you know what I could do" she said.

"Ok, Thank You" I said.

Shortly after getting off the phone with Diana, I realized that Prophetess Blind sent two messages within the group. I opened it.

"How dare you get on here and stir up confusion! I offered you food and you turned it down! I rebuke you in the name of Jesus and I am releasing you from this ministry!" she texted.

Before I could even respond. Prophetess Blind and everyone else exited the group and it was deleted. I couldn't believe this was happening. I was trying to figure out where did I go wrong. What was it that I did that caused all of this. All I asked for was some food.

"Was I wrong for asking? Where exactly did I go wrong? I didn't mean to stir up any confusion" I said to myself.

"Ma, we're hungry. Can you please just call grandma? I know she will come, please call her!" said David.

"Listen David, I'm not sure if you're going to understand but I can't call my mom. The pastor told me to block her awhile back and I haven't spoken to her since then. My mom is angry with me. If I call her, I know she will have something negative to say" I explained.

"But Samantha told me while we were at Renee's house that grandma brought you a chain for Christmas. I don't think she's not mad at you anymore. And what do you mean the pastor told you to block her? Ma, that's your mom! You're not supposed to block her no matter what. It's ok to take some space from her but you're never supposed to block her. Why would the pastor tell you to do something like that? Have she ever blocked her mom?" he said.

"I threw the chain in the garbage. Pastor told me it wouldn't be right to keep it. She told me it would harm me if I did. I just didn't want anything else bad to take place in my life, so I threw it out. She has had complications with her mother in the past but no, she has never blocked her" I said.

"What! You threw the chain grandma brought you in the garbage! Ma, are you crazy?! OMG! What is going on?" he yelled.

"David, calm down! Everything is going to be alright, I know it will" I said.

"Ma, do you see what's going on? Pastor is telling you to do things that she wouldn't even do. She's even asking you to do things that she probably would never do for you or anybody else. That's why I asked you in the car did she have a job. Listen Ma, I know I'm just a kid, but I know when something isn't right; and you haven't been right for a while now. I know that all Pastors have a job. Delivering God's Word is not something they're supposed to get paid for. It's something that they're supposed to do. It's something that's been given from God...like a gift. Ma, this is not right. Is she still bringing the food?" he said.

"No. She just rebuked and released me from the ministry for basically asking for food. I don't know what to do. I stopped talking to everyone because she said they were a distraction regarding this move" I explained.

"So now you're lying to me. You said she was on her way with some food. Ma listen, you didn't know. You thought you were doing the right thing. It's ok but please never do this again. Don't beat yourself up about this. You're a great person. I just don't understand because you know when something isn't right and normally you would say something. Lately you haven't been saying anything. I think you think it's because God would be angry with you. That's how Pastor is making it seem but none of this has to do with God. I don't know much about God but one thing I do know is that, he is not like us. It's not him whose getting angry, it's the Pastor" he said.

Chapter Ten

I couldn't believe my 8-year-old son, was talking like this. Everything he said was true. Although my boys were young, they were very wise and observing. Whether I said anything or not, they knew what was going on. They comprehended very well. I went in my room, locked my door and silently cried.

KNOCK! KNOCK! KNOCK!

"Ma! Open the door! Please! We're hungry! ...that's it! I'm calling grandma myself!" cried David.

I heard him in the other room talking to my mom on his cellphone.

"Hey Grandma, I know it's getting late but me and Keith is hungry. Can you please bring us something to eat? There is no food in our house" he said.

I'm not sure what my mother was saying but I listened as David continue to talk.

"Can you bring me chicken nuggets and French fries? Yes, you can get Keith the same thing as well. My mom is sleeping but can you bring her a large chili" he said.

About 20 minutes later, my mom was knocking on the front door. I still didn't exit from my room. David opened the door and let her in. I listened as my kitchen cabinets opened and closed. I heard my mom go inside the refrigerator and freezer. After about 45 minutes, she left. I waited until David and Keith went to sleep, then I got up and left my room.

I went into the kitchen and look throughout the cabinets and refrigerator. Silently tears stormed from my eyes. My mother came and brought all of us Wendy's. She went grocery shopping and filled my entire kitchen with food. I ate my chili so fast it was crazy, but I was starving. I went back in room, got on my knees and prayed.

"Thank You Jesus! I cried out to you and you came to my rescue. Father, your Word says; *In my distress I called upon the Lord, And cried out to my God; He heard my voice from His temple, And my cry entered His ears. – 2 Samuel 22:7 NKJV* All I can say right now is thank you Father. I didn't think my mother would come but she did. I just want to forgive her and let all of this go. Father God, I do believe that this is her way of showing me that she cares. This is her way of showing me that she loves me. Father, I accept it! Who am I to hold this against her? Father, forgive me and show me how to forgive not only others but myself as well. At this point I'm not sure what to do or where to go. I surrender all to you. I am asking that you direct my every step from this day forward. Not my Will but let your Will be done. In Jesus name, I pray. Amen."

Have mercy on me, O God, have mercy! I look to you for protection. I will hide beneath the shadow of your wings until danger passes by.
-Psalms 57:1 NLT

That night I laid in my bed and stared at the ceiling. I was so tired of crying but there they were…more tears storming from my eyes. This was a long day and I couldn't believe what had taken place. Although my body was tensed, that night I slept in peace. The next morning, I got up and prayed. The moment I got done praying an old friend of mines named Ethen, was on my mind.

Ethen and I worked together at the movie theatre. He used to always tell me stories about how he backslid, and demons attacked him. He would always speak good things about God. He would warn me to repent, get right with God and never turn back to my old ways. Ethen was sick, he was always in and out of the hospital.

I never really knew what was wrong because he only told me bits and pieces about himself. I loved talking and listening to him. Back then, I didn't understand but now I was at a place in my life where I gained a little knowledge regarding God. I'm not sure why he was on my mind this early in the morning, but I didn't hesitate to call him.

"Hey Ethen, Did I wake you?" I said.

"Hey Mika! No, I'm up which is surprising because I'm never up this early. What's going on? You alright?" he said.

Ethen never called me by my full name. He always called me Mika for short.

"I'm not sure if somethings wrong or not. I need to talk, and I really need you to just listen. If I'm wrong about anything, please stop me in my tracks and correct me" I said.

One thing about Ethen is that; he is very honest about any and everything. He never sugar-coated the truth and if you didn't want it, don't ask him.

"Go ahead Mika, I'm listening. Depending on the situation, I will try to be as honest as I know how. If there is something I don't know, I will click over and call my pastor" he said.

"Ok now as you know, I've been a part of this ministry under Prophetess Blind for almost 3 years now. Everything started off right, well at least that's what I thought. Lately…idk but she has been acting weird. She's been throwing a lot of tantrums when things don't go her way. Every time I look up she's talking about someone in the ministry when they don't pay their tithes. She says she's just venting but it seems to me that's she's gossiping.

When someone can't do something her way, all hell breaks loose. I try to make her happy because she's my leader. To me there is a certain level of respect that is to be given when it comes to her and Elder Blind. Now as far as this move, she says it's the Will of God, but nothing is going right and then I'm paying for everything. I told her the other day, I might not be able to because I wouldn't be left with anything. She tells me to take that up with God. I really felt like she was basically saying that's not her problem. Recently, she called a fast and I ran out of food. For 3 days me and my babies didn't have any food. I decided to ask her for help. At first, she stated that she would help then she texted me at 3am in the morning stating that an unexpected bill came up. Now I'm rebuked and released from the ministry. She got on Facebook and told everyone God is going to bless them for being obedient during the fast. I responded that God will still bless those who are unable to continue with the fast. Her and Diana got mad and went off on me. Me and my babies were hungry. If it wasn't for my mother who she told me to block, I wouldn't have a house full of food right now. I just don't understand where I went wrong" I explained.

"Mika, you didn't do anything wrong. You asked for help, that's what you did! Due to her misusing the tithes and offerings for her own personal needs, she was unable to help you. Now she is playing victim and got you feeling guilty like it's all your fault. This is what happens when we don't know who God is. We run to our pastors and people who can fail us at any time. They can lie and misuse us at any given time, but God would never fail us. He would never lead us astray and mistreat us. It's been 3 years Mika, whatever this woman is operating in, she got you in deep. That's alright though because we serve a mighty God and it ain't never too late. Be glad that she rebuked and released you. God has finally set you free! Be glad! Mika, rejoice and repent for praising her and not God. Repent for not seeking God first yet placing her before him. Mika listen, It sounds like some demonic type of stuff to me, but I don't want to blaspheme. If you want me to, I can call my pastor on three-way. She doesn't have to know anything about you or what you just shared with me. We gone let the holy spirit lead her and pray for you" he said.

"Yes, that's fine. You can call her" I replied.

Ethen clicked over and called his pastor. He added her to the line where we all was on one accord.

"Hey Pastor, a good friend of mine needs prayer this morning. She's on the phone right now as we speak" he said.

"Hey, ok what's your name baby?" asked Ethen Pastor.

"Shamika" I responded.

"Is there anything you want me to pray about specifically?" she asked.

"Yes. This move to North Carolina" I responded.

As Ethen pastor begin to pray, there was this feeling in me. I slowly begin to feel relieved. It was as if a burden had been lifted. She prayed for about 10 minutes. When she got done she shared something with me.

"You are a true woman after God's heart. You love God so much and you would do anything for him. God has you in his hands, he's got you covered. For some time now, some people have been pulling on you and forcing you to do things that are not of God. There are still somethings that God wants you to complete. There are still somethings in which you know you need to let go. It will all be on God's timing, not yours or anyone else. You know when something isn't right because God has blessed you with his discernment. You are going to be alright. Keep running after God, keep him first above all and don't ever stop praising him" she said.

After hearing Ethen pastor speak these words to me, I felt that feeling that I felt the day I got baptized. It was a warm, comforting feeling and it made me feel free.

"Ok, pastor I will talk to you later. Mika, are you still there?" asked Ethen.

"Yes, I'm here" I said.

"Ok. I just want you to know that I'm here if you ever need me. If I were you I would be somewhere all up in the face of God praising him and only him. Mika, it's alright that all of this happened. God has been showing you this woman from day one. You didn't know and even if you did, you probably weren't sure. Trust me when I say, she knew though. She picked up something in your spirit and has been using you, instead of helping you. You must be careful Mika, there are false prophets everywhere. Now that you do know repent, pray and lean strictly on God. Stay in his Word and let him lead you. Don't hesitate to call me when you need me" he said.

"Ok, Thank You" I said.

And many false prophets will appear and will deceive many people. -Matthew 24:11 NLT

That night before bed, I sat in the middle of my bedroom floor. I cried out to God like never before. I repented for all my sins. All the things I did, I didn't do, I kept running back to, I kept seeking and all of which I refused to let go. I confessed it all and I left it all in his hands.

After confessing, I begin to praise and worship God for never leaving me and for loving me enough to wait on me. I thanked him for his grace, favor and mercy upon me. I thanked him for loving me in a time where I knew nothing about love. I know I cried numerous times before, but this was a different type of cry. I begin to feel that warm comforting feeling again. I knew deep down inside that a change was about to take place in my life.

I got up went into the bathroom and washed my face. While in the bathroom, I heard my phone ringing. I didn't wonder who it could be. I was so tired of overthinking, wondering and trying to figure everything out. I was done with everything. I completely handed it all over to God. I walked back into my room to see who was calling me so late. It was Prophetess Blind, I answered.

"Hey, you busy?" she asked.

"I'm getting ready to go to bed" I responded.

"Listen, God placed it on my heart to call and talk to you. To see what your problem is" she said.

"Really? Just a day ago you rebuked and released me. Now you're saying God told you to call me. Is it really God or is this you?" I said sarcastically.

"First off, I would never rebuke and release you. I am your spiritual mother and you're my daughter. Shamika, I love you, but you will not stir up any confusion in this ministry" she said.

"Log back on Facebook, reopen that group and tell them what you're telling me now. How exactly did I stir up confusion? All I did was ask for food and made a statement that God will still bless those who are basically less fortunate. God is very understanding, unlike you" I said.

"This conversation is between me and you. I don't have to go back and do anything. You better repent for talking to your leader like this. Repent! Right now! God will curse you!" she yelled.

"I already did. You say this conversation is between me and you. If that's the case, how does Diana know I quit my job? I never shared anything personal with her" I said.

"She is my armorbearer! I don't have to explain anything to you! Shamika you better Repent! God is going to curse you if you don't!" she said.

"Right but I have to tell you everything though. Any who, I talk to Ethen today and his pastor prayed for me. She said some people have been pulling on me and forcing me to do things that are not of God…What's really going on?" I said.

"Oh my God! That's where all this confusion is coming from! You're talking to other people that are speaking against what God is saying. You are constantly being disobedient and getting yourself wrapped deeply in a bunch of mess. You had no business talking to his pastor let alone, letting her pray over you. I am your pastor! God has placed you under my wing! You are out of order! Repent! Right now! God will curse you if you don't!" she yelled again.

"Listen, I told you I already did. I'm getting ready to go to bed" I said nonchalantly.

"Do you still want to be a part of this ministry?" she asked.

"You rebuked and released me. I'm not sure what to do at this moment" I responded.

"Shamika, God is giving you another chance" she said.
"I am getting ready for bed. I will talk to you some other time" I said.

"Ok, well you are more than welcomed to continue to get on the prayer line. Good night, I love you. I will talk to you soon baby girl" she said.

I really didn't know what to believe anymore. I wasn't putting anymore thought into this. I was strictly taking everything before God. I desired to hear from him. The following week, I decided not to get on the prayer line. I decided to read the Word of God and spend time with him instead. Thursday came around and I noticed that it was a little after 7pm. Prophetess Blind was never late when it was time to counsel me on Thursdays. I doubt if she did but maybe she forgot, I decided to call her.

"Hey, are we still on for tonight?" I asked.

"Yes, I'm sorry. I got a little behind time. So, what do you want to talk about today?" she asked.

For her to ask me this was awkward. Any other time she would jump right into asking me things about my mother. I was shocked and really didn't know what to talk about. I decided to ask about the move, I really wanted to get down to the bottom of this.

"Do I really have to move to North Carolina with you all?" I asked.

"You know what if you're not ready, you do not have to come. I wouldn't want you to get down there and panic. If you want to stay, you can stay and when you're ready, then you can come" she responded.

"Ok well I'm going to stay. I feel so much better now. I felt like I had to do it, or else God would be angry with me" I said.

"Oh no baby girl! If you don't want to come, you don't have too. God will understand. If me and my family must go alone, then we will just go alone. This is something God wants me to do. I'm sorry for trying to bring you all along with me and experience my blessings" she said.

"Aw ok" I responded.

"After today this will be the last time counseling session. I have tried to do everything that I can for you, but nothing seems to work. I think that maybe you should seek professional counseling, maybe that will help you" she said.
"What do you mean?" I asked.

"You're just unable to make up your mind. It's too much indecisiveness and overthinking. You're unstable, and it comes from your past relationship with your mother. It's far too deep for me to get to and help you" she said.

"Oh wow! So, what should I do?" I asked.

"Talk to God about it baby girl. Have you thought about remaining apart of this ministry?" she asked.

"I'm not sure. I just want to stay in the face of God for now" I said.

"Ok, well let me know. I have to go now. I have to get on the prayer line. Before I go, I would like to talk to you about something" she said.

"Ok, what's that?" I asked.

"I just want you to know that you don't have to buy me a new stove or pay the moving fee. However, can you please make sure you pay your tithes and offering though?" she said.

"Ok" I responded.

I can't believe that she basically called me crazy. She had the nerve to tell me that I need additional help that she couldn't provide. I wonder did she just figure this out or did she know this already? My situation is not that bad. I know for a fact that it's nothing too hard for God to handle. I was starting to believe that something was wrong with her.

I'm not sure if she realizes it but from the day I met her, she has been saying things and even preaching sermons, that she doesn't even abide by herself. I'm trying to figure out when was she going to tell me that this move is basically not the Will of God. No! what really took the cake is when she asked me to still pay my tithes and offerings...after the fact that she just told me that I'm crazy and she can't help me. That's not even including the fact that I just told her I'm not sure if I still want to be a part of the ministry.

The next morning, I got up to a missed call from Faith. I called her back and we laughed about many things as usual. I wanted to hear her opinion regarding everything that was going on with me. I knew that I could share this with her. I explained to Faith everything that I talked about with Ethen and his pastor. I even told her about the conversation during counseling with Prophetess Blind.

"OMG! Shamika, are you alright?" she asked.

"I'm not sure. I think I am. It feels like I'm better now" I responded.

"Shamika, I've always wanted to say something, but I knew that I couldn't. You were just so deep in everything that this lady was telling you. It's like nothing else mattered. I heard about you blocking your mom. I didn't want you to block me if I would've said something. I knew the best thing to do was to just stick by your side, act normal and continue to pray for you" she explained.

"Wow! I'm sorry Faith. Normally I would speak my mind but it's like I couldn't say anything" I said.

"It's cool, Shamika. I know a lot of people that has been through similar situations like this. I just never thought it would be my own cousin. It hurts to know that this lady has been getting over on you. Without you knowing, you're thinking that you were doing the right thing. Do you still talk to her?" she said.

"I just recently spoke to her last night" I said.

"Shamika, please don't think I'm trying to tell you what to do but I really think you should block her. I just don't want you to find yourself going back into something that was never healthy for you to begin with" she explained.

"I never thought of it that way. However, I do need some space from all of this. You know what you have a point. Let me call you right back" I said.

After getting off the phone with Faith, I logged on to Facebook. I blocked Prophetess Blind, her mother and kids. I also blocked Diana and Terry. I didn't block Malcom and Anna. Even though Mona was Prophetess Blind sister, I didn't block her either. I felt like we had been friends before all of this and so we should remain friends after this.

Awhile after going on a blocking spree, Prophetess Blind called me, but I didn't answer. She called numerously 10 more times, then she stopped. About 5 minutes later, I received a message on Facebook from Mona.

"Hey Shamika, do you have a problem with my sister?" she asked.

Now, Mona was a very sweet person. Although me and her rarely talked, she was a great friend in times of need. I didn't look at this message and think that she was coming off in a bad way. However, I knew the moment Prophetess Bind stopped calling me, she called Mona crying and played the victim. As bad as I wanted to explain to Mona what happened, I knew that she would believe her sister over me, regardless of the situation.

"Hey Mona, No. I don't have a problem with your sister" I responded.

"Ok, so what's going on because she just called me crying. She's worried about you and she said you blocked her" she replied.

"I think that maybe you should talk to your sister about everything once she calms down" I responded.

"Ok" she said.

Later that day, Mona deleted me off Facebook. To be honest I really didn't care. Mona and I rarely talked and although she wasn't a bad person; her loyalty was with Miya. She didn't care much for me which explains why it didn't take much for her to delete me. I believe that's what she always wanted to do, she just didn't have a good enough reason to do so. I was glad I didn't explain to her what happened. I knew she wasn't going to believe anything I said. It would have been a waste of my time.

Laying in my bed, I begin to cry. It was like a part of me felt free but the other half of me felt guilty. I really believed in my mind that I did something wrong. I replayed everything that took place from the day I joined the ministry. It didn't add up as to why I felt guilty, I just did. Still crying, I received a message on Facebook from Malcolm.

"Hey Shamika, Can I call you?" he asked.

"Yea" I replied.

Without hesitation Malcolm called me.

"Shamika is everything alright? Are you still apart of the ministry?" he asked.

"Malcolm, listen to me Prophetess Blind is not right. She has been manipulating me and doing a lot of dreadful things no one knows about. This whole move thing is not God's Will, please don't go. I'm sorry for dragging you in this but I didn't know" I cried.

"Shamika, listen I'm not sure what's going on. One thing I do know is that the spiritual welfare in this ministry is strong. I have never experienced anything like this before. Now as far as moving, I don't want to go either Shamika, but I am trusting God. My family have been telling me not to go as well. A lot has been going on, but I am trusting God. Prophetess Blind is an Amazing woman. She is our spiritual mother, so please just calm down and rethink this. Listen, I'm at work right now but I will call you back later...calm down" he said.

"Malcolm, I'm sorry! Don't go! Please don't move to North Carolina! It's not God's Will! None of this is right!" I cried.

"Ok...Ok. I will call you back.... calm down" he whispered.

I was crying like crazy. I couldn't even think straight enough to explain to Malcolm all that had been going on. From the way he was talking, Prophetess Blind manipulation had already taken place on him. He was covering for her and didn't even fully know what he was covering for.

He reminded me of myself. I begin to realize how I was reacting when people tried to warn me. There were things that I couldn't see regarding her, that others could see. However, due to me being blind, hurt and vulnerable, I consistently covered for her and isolated myself from everyone.

The next morning, I got up, prayed and meditated on God's Word. I decided to call Miya and have a talk with her. After all, she did tell me if I ever needed her to call.

"Hey Miya, you busy?" I asked.

"Hey Shamika, I'm on my way to work but we can talk" she said.

"I wanted to share something with. I would like your honest opinion about it. I need you to just listen" I said.

"Ok" she responded.

I told Miya everything that happened with me all while I was a part of the ministry. I even explained to her how Mona responded and deleted me off Facebook. She listened clearly to everything but then I realized she begin to compare this situation to what happened between me and her.

"Shamika listen, I am going to be honest with you. I think that you were wrong for blocking her even after ya'll had a decent conversation. As far as Mona, I'm not sure why she would delete you. I don't understand though because if you consider her your friend, whether that's her sister or not, why wouldn't you tell her what's going on" she said.

"I blocked her because I needed space from her and this whole situation. I didn't tell Mona because I knew she would react the way she did" I responded.

"Shamika, it doesn't matter. You can't just block somebody out without saying anything. I think you should've at least told her before you did that, to have a clear understanding. Now as far as everything else, I just think that maybe you felt used and hurt. I know you may not want to hear this right now but Shamika what goes around comes around. Karma is nothing to be played with. You hurt and used a lot of people and didn't even care. Hell, you did it to me and now you calling me. You just have to be careful with how you treat people" she said.

"Are you serious right now? Miya, I'm calling you because back when you reached out to me in December, you told me to call you if I ever needed you. I need you to listen and give me your honest feedback" I said.

"Ok Shamika and that's what I'm doing" she said.

"No, you're not. You're telling me about my past and who I hurt. Now you talking about me, you and what happened between us" I said.

"No, no, no. I am just trying to give you an example of where I'm coming from to better help you understand" she said.

"Whoever said I didn't understand? I'm listening to you for feedback regarding this church situation and you start talking about what happened with us. Listen, please don't tell anyone that we talked about this. Let's just keep this between me and you. Hopefully, we can build our friendship again, starting with trust first" I said.

"Ok, I feel you. I won't say anything to anyone. I'm about to clock in. I will talk to you later" she said.

"Ok" I responded.

It was pointless calling Miya. She still hasn't forgiven me from something that happened 5 years ago. Every time we had a conversation somehow it led to what happened between me and her. She was always trying to get an answer out of me. I would never be able to explain why I hurt anyone. The only explanation there would be; Is that I was hurt myself. Everyone I came across got a dose of the hurt I carried. Unintentionally, it spread like a disease that I would never be able to cure.

Later that day, I decided to take my babies for a walk to the park. Just doing something so simple made me feel free. All I ever did was go to work and come straight home. While walking to the park, I got a slight headache on the right side of my head. I didn't eat anything, due to me not having an appetite. After about an hour and a half at the park, we headed back home. The headache had gotten stronger. I decided to eat something so that it would go away but it didn't. It got worse and very painful. I decided to lay down for a while. While resting, I received a long text from Diana.

"You are evil, and you operate in the spirit of Jezebel! I knew all along you were evil and twisted from the day I met you. You're going around telling lies so that people can feel sorry for you, all over some lunchmeat. All because you decided to quit your job. You should've thought about that before you quit. Your motives are wrong and have been since day one. It's not my or Prophetess Blind responsibility to do anything for you! How dare you go around and stir up confusion?! You Jezebel! But guess what ain't no Ahab over on this end! God will curse you and everything you do" she said.

Who is Jezebel? Short passage to better help the reader understand Author.

Jezebel was the daughter of Ethbaal; King of the Sidonians. She was the wife of King Ahab and a worshipper of Baal. She was very evil, manipulating and controlling. You can find more information regarding Jezebel, King Ahab and The Prophet Elijah in the book of 1 Kings 16:31 NLT and so forth.

Reading Diana's message, I was shocked she was saying these things to me. However, I was very calm when I responded back to her. I was already going through too much to allow anything extra add to it.

"Wow! So, you mean to tell me all this time that I've been operating in the spirit of Jezebel? No one said anything about it and neither was anyone praying for me. What ever happened to the praying warriors? You say you knew this since day one. Were you praying for me since day one?" I replied.

"You heard what I said! Ain't no Ahab over on this end. I just hope you're ready because God is going to curse you. There is no turning back when he does! No need to reply to this message. Just take note of what I said. You will be cursed!" she said.

"I'm sorry that you feel the way you feel about me. I barely even know you for you to be so hostile towards me. I have done nothing more but give my all and try to help in every way I know how. When it comes to this ministry, my motives were right behind everything I ever did and said. I never asked for anything, all I ever wanted was more of God in return of everything I ever did. However, the one time I ask for food, this is what I get in return. I don't care what you say… If I don't know nothing else about myself, one thing I do know is that I do not operate in the spirit of Jezebel. Furthermore, I wish nothing but the best for you, your family and the ministry as you all continue to move forward" I replied.

I couldn't believe the things Diana had texted me. I hadn't spoken to Prophetess Blind; however, I decided to screenshot Diana messages and send them to her. When I texted Prophetess Blind, she instantly replied.

"So, you're going around lying telling people that I used you Shamika! Really! Don't you ever text or call my phone again!" she said.

At first, I was confused because I didn't recall telling anyone that she used me. I, then, thought about Miya and our whole conversation.

"She either told Mona and Mona told Prophetess Blind or Prophetess Blind called. I can't believe Miya, I should've expected this from her though. Whenever I discussed anything with her, she misinterpreted everything. We just came down to an agreement that we weren't going to tell anyone what we talked about. We just discussed building trust. Why would she do that and why would she tell her I said she used me? Those were her words not mine" I said to myself.

I didn't know what was going on. Things just kept happening and adding to what I was already going through. I just wanted out and I didn't want to talk or be around anyone but God. I changed my number that night so that no one apart of that ministry could get in contact with me.

I deactivated my Facebook page only until I was able to get my thoughts straight. I was angry, hurt, broken, confused, and vulnerable. All of this just added to everything I was already suffering from within. I just couldn't take it anymore.

The next day, David went with his best friend and wasn't coming back until 10pm that night. It was only me and Keith in the house. I decided that since David was gone, I would spend some time with my baby. I had our entire day planned on fun activities. Before I could get the day started my head started to hurt.

It was weird because this headache was only on the right side of my head. I didn't understand what was wrong. I made sure I ate and drunk plenty of water, but it only got worse. I started to get dizzy while playing Keith. I decided to turn on his favorite cartoons. I pulled out his toys for him while I went in my room and laid down.

When I laid down, the headache grew stronger. It hurted for me to lay my head on my pillow. It was painful for me to move period. I tossed and turned trying to find comfort in being still. I laid flat on my back in the middle of my bed with my eyes closed. Tears raced from my shut eyes as I begin to pray.

"Jesus…please…help…me" I said.

It was difficult for me to move my mouth and talk. At 8pm, Keith came in my room and pounced on top of me.

"Mommy, I'm hungry" he said.

When Keith jumped on me, my body was in sufferance. It felt like I had been beaten. I couldn't move, talk and I could barely open my eyes.

"Come...lay...with...ma...ma" I said as I patted my bed.

"Ok, mommy!" he said.

I could hear Keith run in his room, clean the toys up and turn off the TV. He then, came and climbed in bed with me. He snuggled right under me and went to sleep in no time. Although, Keith just made 3 years old, he was very clever and advertence. It hurt me that my baby had to go to sleep on an empty stomach, however there was not much that I could do.

After laying down for hours, my head was still aching. At this point, the headache had spread all over my head. It had got so terrible that it felt like my heart was pumping from my brain. Headed to the bathroom, I slowly got up only to hit the floor. Not only was my body afflicted, it was unsubstantial as well.

Slowly raising up off the floor, I held on tight as my walls led me to the bathroom. I stood close in front of my mirror and opened my eyes slowly. My eyes were dark bloodshot red. It tormented me just to open them and look at myself.

I opened my medicine cabinet and I took 3 different pill medications without being able to see what they were. I didn't care I just really wanted this pain to go away. Still holding onto my walls before I walked out of the bathroom, I looked at myself again. I heard a soft voice whisper to me;

"You're going to be alright. You have nothing to worry about. Lay down and get some rest. I promise to comfort you in this time of distress"

Even when I walk through the darkest valley, I will not be afraid, for you are close beside me. Your rod and your staff protect and comfort me. -Psalms 23:4 NLT

I didn't know where the voice came from or who it was, but I did what it told me to do. Before I knew it, 10pm arrived and David was knocking at the door. When I opened the front door to let him in, the big smile on his face instantly turned into tears.

"Oh ma! Look at your eyes! Are you alright!" he cried.
"Try...not...to...look...at...me...I... will...be...ok...I...pro...mise" I said.

"Ok, where is Keith?" he asked.

"sleep" I responded.

"Ma, I'm about to pray for you right now!" he yelled.

"Yes…pray…for…me" I said.

That night I tossed and turned constantly. I kept hearing David cry out to God.

"God, please keep my mom! Please! I love her, and I can't lose her. I need her, and I just want her to be happy. I want her to be herself again! Please help her right now! Hold her in your arms! Father, I don't think she can talk and her eyes are scary! I never seen her like this before…I'm so scared and I'm doing what she told me to do when I get scared. I'm talking to you about it. Please don't take my mom away from me and Keith! We need her! Please just help her!" he cried.

After a couple more toss and turns, the headache went away, and I was able to rest. I was unable to move my mouth for 3 days. For 1 week, I was unable to move. For 2 weeks straight the painful headaches came and went at separate times. Every time I felt it coming on, I started praising and worshipping God.

Once everything went away completely. I was furious about what happened to me and I wanted everyone to know. I wanted Prophetess Blind to burn in hell one minute and the next minute I wanted to go kill her and Elder Blind. For a week straight, I thought about so many ways to get revenge. I wanted her to feel what I felt. However, deep down inside I knew I could never handle her better than God.

> *I will take revenge; I will pay them back. In due time their feet will slip. Their day of disaster will arrive, and their destiny will overtake them. -Deuteronomy 32:35 NLT*

The following weeks were the complete opposite, I cried out to God every day and night.

"Father God, lately I've been angry alright…and I just don't know what to do. I want to do something about this so bad. I know that no one can handle me or this situation better than you. I feel free now that I'm no longer imprisoned, manipulated and controlled by Prophetess Blind. However, I still feel like a slave to unforgiveness and anger. Father, this just isn't me. I'm not sure who I am but I know for a fact this isn't who I am. I am not one to sit up and hold grudges and seek revenge. I just want to let all this go. I don't want to be a slave to anyone or anything. Father, should anyone else use me, let it be you and only you. All I want at this point in my life is you. What do I have to do to get more of you? Where should I start? Can you teach me your ways? I promise that I will obey and keep them. Father your word says; *Teach me your ways, O*

Lord, that I may live according to your truth! Grant me purity of heart, so that I may honor you. -Psalms 86:11 NLT

Father, I need you more than anything right now. I just want more of you. I'm yearning for the day to come where I can forgive wholeheartedly. Father, all I ask is that your deliver me from these chains of unforgiveness, anger, hurt and lust. I am tired of waking up sweating and itching for sex. I am worth more than this, I know I am. My body belongs to you. My body belongs to my husband. The man that you have reserved and set apart for me. Father, can you show me what love is. I'm tired of waiting around for my mother and everybody else to love me. I desire for you to overflow me with your love. Father, drown me in your love to the point where I truly understand and begin to love myself first. Father God, who am I? and what is your Will for me? Father…Just please! Can you guide me? Forgive me for seeking love and attention in all the wrong places. I damaged myself even more without even realizing it. I repent right now in Jesus name for all my sins. I ask that you forgive me and please help me to forgive myself. Grant me more of your Grace to submit to you. I desire to remain obedient and faithful to you. Forgive me for those that I hurt in my past knowingly and unintentionally. Have mercy upon their souls, so that they may find it in their heart to forgive me as well. Father, from this day forward I surrender all to you. I vow to never place anything or anyone above or before you ever again. I vow to come strictly to you and talk to you first about every and anything. I no longer want to be ashamed, isolate myself or hide anything from you. Whatever I do, I will forever run to you and share it with you. No longer will I be ashamed and isolate myself. Father, I trust you with my life… you created me. I know for a fact, a couple of weeks ago that if it wasn't for you, I'd be dead and gone. Father God, you kept me…you spared my life…you waited patiently for me…you led me through the darkness, you were my light and my strong tower even when I didn't know what was going on. You stood strong right by my side and endured with me through it all. Now here we are alone together. Father, all I ask for is two things…and that's more of you and a pure heart. In Jesus mighty name, I pray. Amen" I prayed.

Moving forward I continued to pray, read the bible, and worship God, 3 times a day. At 6am, 5pm and 8pm Sunday through Saturday I got before God and talked to him about everything. As time went on, I wanted to know who Prophetess Blind was and what was she seeking. I wanted to know why I felt the way I did that night I experienced what seemed like death. I talked to God about it and he spoke. His voice was so soft and clear.

"Starting tomorrow, for 3 days drink nothing but water and read the book of 1 Samuel" he said.

"Ok" I responded.

Getting to know God was amazing. My relationship with him, was like no other. I was never good with expressing myself and being open to anyone. With God it was different. I emptied myself before him every chance I got. There were times where I asked him certain things and he was silent. I would grow impatient.

I would even talk to him about that because I felt like he was ignoring me. It was in those times that I realized it wasn't that he was ignoring me. He heard my every prayer. It was in his silence that he had shown me myself. He was only doing what I asked of him to do. He was purifying my heart. A lot of things deeply rooted within me had begun to come up and out.

During the fast, I thought God was going to show me Prophetess Blind in my dreams. Overtime I realized that was his way of speaking to me. This time was different though. On the third day, right before I finished the last chapter of 1 Samuel, he spoke to me.

"Shamika, Winter operates in the spirit of King Saul. She has been moving based off her own understanding and using my Word in vain. Just like Saul, she seeks to build her own Kingdom. You have done no wrong. Trust me and know that my Grace is sufficient" he said.

When God shared this information with me. I praised him.

"Father, I thank you for answering my prayer and setting me free but please don't hurt her. Forgive her for doing this to me and others. Forgive her for using your Word in vain. Father, maybe somewhere in her past it was taught and done to her. Maybe she believes she's doing the right thing. I know she hurt me and misused me, yet I would never wish this upon anyone else. Set everyone apart of that ministry free. Father, please keep Malcolm. I know if I say something he won't listen. Father, forgive me for dragging him along, I didn't know" I said.

"Do not worry about Malcolm. I will keep him. Pray for him" he said.

"Thank you" I responded.

Weeks passed by and before I knew it I received my tax refund. I kept my word and budgeted every dollar I spent. Since I still wasn't working, I paid all my bills 6 months in advance. I was even able to pay my light bill in full. After taking care of what was most important, I was left with $5,500.

The car dealership came and picked up my car. I was walking everywhere I needed to go. Thank God for my place of residence because I didn't have to travel far at all. Laundromats, schools, grocery stores, restaurants and public transportation was very convenient for me.

One morning while walking home from dropping my babies off to school. I received an email from Prophetess Blind.

"Shamika, are you alright?" she wrote.

I read the email, but I didn't respond. Instead I blocked her email from sending me messages. After reading that message I started having minor headaches again. I prayed, and it went away. The following week, she emailed me again from a different email address. This time I responded.

"Shamika, I love you. Are you alright?" she wrote.

"Leave me alone" I responded.

"I'm concerned about you. I'm sorry for everything" she said.

"Are you concerned about me or are you trying to confirm if whether I'm going through or not?" I asked.

I asked Prophetess Blind this question because back then when she rebuked and released a member, she would always repeat;

"I know they're going through. Ain't nothing going good for them. They're going through hell right now"

I instantly replayed that in my mind and felt that's why she was reaching out. I also knew right then and there that I hadn't forgiven her. I doubt if she was concerned. Although she repeated that she loved me, I knew she really didn't mean it. She presented a counterfeit love to draw close to me. She knew that I didn't know what Love was to begin with and so she took full advantage of me. I just didn't want to have anything to do with her.

"Shamika, I love you. I am really concerned" she replied.

"Well if you're that concerned then talk to God about it. Let him show you if I'm alright or not" I responded.

"Shamika, I'm sorry" she said.

"Sorry for what? for allowing Diana to talk to me the way she did?" I said.

"No. Diana is my armorbearer. She had every right to say what she said. You were out of order" she said.

"Wait a minute! You mean to tell me she had every right as your armorbearer to talk to me that way? Whatever happened to armorbearers is only suppose fight in the spirit? Explain to me how I was out of order for asking for food" I said.

"There you go throwing rocks again" she replied.

"I'm not throwing rocks at anyone, you're crazy. You know something... I dreamed of all of this before it happened, but I didn't know what was going on" I said.

"Whatever Shamika! Stop lying! You didn't dream of anything" she said.

"I guess that since I'm not a part of your ministry anymore that means God can't bless me or speak to me, huh? You know that night I didn't have food, my mom came over and filled my house with food. The one you told me to block. First, you stated that the things she does are love languages, then, you turn around and tell me that basically she's harmful to me. Which one is it?" I said.

"I never said that you couldn't ask her for anything" she said.

"You basically did by telling me to block her but it's not your fault...I should've known better" I responded.

After I responded, I blocked her new email and created me a new email address. Now she was unable to contact me. That night I had a long talk with God about everything that took place that day. I asked him to deal with my heart more regarding unforgiveness. I realized my responses to her wasn't appropriate. What she did wasn't right but just because she was wrong didn't mean I had to respond in such way. It just wasn't in me to be like that. I didn't want to be evil. I didn't want to walk around deceived and treat people the way she treated me.

That night before bed, I experienced another minor headache. I was starting to believe that every time I talked to her, it caused me to get a headache out of nowhere. This wasn't a normal headache. It lasted almost a week before it went away. Throughout the week, I decided to search you-tube and google, on information about various kinds of headaches.

One thing led to another and before I knew it, I was reading about witchcraft and cults. I watched this one video on you-tube about a man who was a part of a cult. He didn't know it until he broke free. He stated that his pastor came off so loving and caring when he first met him. Later down the line, he started to get very controlling. He started using the members to draw other members just to carry out his plan for the ministry. This man misused all the tithes for his own personal needs. The man explained that when this pastor preached God's Word, you would think that he was one of God, but he wasn't.

He explained that it got so bad in the church that members started to commit suicide. His pastor would make the members feel horrible if they went out and enjoyed themselves. When the man decided to break free he didn't tell his pastor, he just left. He experienced major headaches and was tortured almost every night with witchcraft dreams. It wasn't until he sought help that he realized that he was a part of a demonic cult. His counselor explained to him that if he hadn't come any sooner, he would've died.

After viewing this video, I realized this was the exact same thing that I just experienced. I cried and begin to praise God because he kept me through it all.

"Father God, I thank you for keeping those people that struggles from once being a part of a cult. Father, heal me, deliver me and use me for your Glory. Strengthen me and grant me more of your Grace to share my testimony. I desire for people to know that it was you who kept me, blessed me, and equipped me to serve your purpose. Father, I just want people to know that no matter what their situation is they can always run to you. I know that if you spared my life, you would do the same for anyone who choose to surrender all to you. I am so glad that I endured something so painful. I am glad I went through it all with you by my side. Please use me as you please to set others free. Father, grant me your Grace to learn from this and not grow bitter. Not my Will, but let your Will be done. In Jesus name, I pray. Amen" I prayed.

So be truly glad. There is wonderful joy ahead, even though you must endure many trails for a little while. -1 Peter 1:6 NLT

From that day forward, I accepted everything that I endured in my life. The more time I spent with God, I realized that he can use any hardship for his Glory. With everything that had taken place in my life, I stopped and choose to focus strictly on one thing, I chose God.

I chose to strictly keep my eyes on him no matter what. This was the best choice I had ever made in my life. I watched him as he moved in. I watched as he fixed every broken piece in me and molded me into his image. I embraced his many blessings in everything, according to his Will that I accomplished.

As time proceeded, I went back to school and graduated with my certificate in Child Psychology. I started a small affordable daycare business. I wrote, edit and self-published my first book called "Face Yourself". I traveled for the first time in my life to Las Vegas. After years of applying, I was finally hired to work for the City of Chicago. However, now I understand that if it's according to God's Will and it's for me, it's going to happen on his timing. My mom and I talked and we're rebuilding our relationship. Ellis and Keith reunited. Keith now knows and spends time with his family on his father side. Karter is a working progress and is trying to do right by Keith. Kris and David bond has grown strong and more beautiful than ever.

I spoke to Malcolm in October 2017, around the time I published my book. He was still praising Prophetess Blind and calling her his spiritual mother. He stated that they never relocated to North Carolina because Prophetess Blind said God pushed the date back.

The truth of the matter is, they didn't go because she didn't have any money. I'm sure she told everyone what she wanted them to know and left it at that. However, I couldn't tell Malcolm any of this. I listened as he shared these things with me. My advice to him was to keep God first no matter what.

You see I couldn't just burst out and imprecate Prophetess Blind. What she did to me didn't necessary mean she was going to do it to Malcolm. She had a suave way of manipulating each member of her ministry accordingly. However, I serve a mighty God. I know for a fact that if God kept me, there's no doubt in my mind that he wouldn't keep Malcolm.

And we know that God causes everything to work together for the good of those who love God and are called according to his purpose for them. -Romans 8:28 NLT

Over the course of time, I realized that Prophetess Blind had been deceived. Her true intentions were nothing more than to demolish me. Everything I accomplished after breaking free is what was truly God's Will for me. Today, I live on led by no other than God. What I've encountered was pernicious and marvel...But God Kept Me.

And so, I walk in the Lord's presence as I live here on earth! -Psalms 116:9 NLT

Special letter to reader

I appreciate you for taking the time out to read my book. I pray that my testimony inspired, motivated, and encouraged you in some way. I pray that no matter what it is, minor or major; You seek God first about it and believe that he will guide and keep you through it all. Thank You. May God continue to Bless you.

Yours Truly with Love, Shamika King

Trust in the Lord with all your heart; do not depend on your own understanding. Seek his Will in all you do, and he will show you which path to take. -Proverbs 3:5-6 NLT

Contact Information

Podcast: Anchor.fm/nourishinspirations

<u>Other books by Shamika King</u>

Face Yourself
What They Can't See Affects Them
Nourish Inspirations

*All books are available on **amazon.com/author/shamikaking***

Made in the USA
Middletown, DE
08 June 2022

66757352R00186